MAYA MEDICINE

Maya
Medicine

TRADITIONAL HEALING IN YUCATAN

Marianna Appel Kunow

UNIVERSITY OF NEW MEXICO PRESS   ALBUQUERQUE

LIBRARY OF CONGRESS CATALOGING-IN-PUBLICATION DATA

Kunow, Marianna Appel, 1958—
    Maya Medicine : traditional healing in Yucatán / Marianna Appel Kunow.—1st ed.
        p. cm.
Includes bibliographical references and index.
    ISBN 0-8263-2864-4 (cloth : alk. paper)
    1. Mayas—Medicine—Mexico—Yucatán (State).
    2. Mayas—Ethnobotany—Mexico—Yucatán (State).
    3. Healers—Mexico—Pisté. I. Title
        F1435.3M4 K86 2003
        615.8'8'097265—dc21

                                                    2002011042

BOOK DESIGN: Mina Yamashita

Contents

List of Tables

List of Illustrations

Acknowledgements

This book would not have become a reality
without the curers of Yucatan and their families.
I appreciate everything they shared with me,
and I dedicate this book to them. Special thanks
also go to all those who supported my research
and believed in the idea of this book, especially
Kim and Ana Sofia Kunow, Carla Appel, John Nesbitt,
Eleuterio Po'ot Yah, Anne S. Bradburn, Dr. Victoria R.
Bricker, Dr. Mary Elizabeth Smith, Dr. William Balée,
Dr. Steven Darwin, and Dr. E. Wyllys Andrews.

CHAPTER ONE
Introduction and Setting

Introduction

A surprising number of practitioners of traditional Maya medicine are con-
sulted by the townspeople of Pisté, a small town located in the center of the
northern half of Mexico's Yucatan peninsula. The curers I have come to know
use a variety of indigenous and introduced plants in their practices. They utilize
these abundant natural resources along with Western medicine and traditional
rituals that include magical elements. My goal in this book is to examine the
process of curing from the time the curers begin to acquire their skills, through
the administration of treatments. These treatments will be examined in depth.
I link the ethnographic present to the past by examining the relationship
between current curing practices and their colonial antecedents.

Pisté is not an extraordinarily traditional town. As the town nearest the ruins of Chichén Itzá, it is neither isolated nor removed from acculturative influences. However, the curers practicing in the area share a tradition of plant
use and ethnomedicine that is remarkably homogeneous given that not all
the curers and not all their teachers are natives of Pisté. There is a body of information on useful and medicinal plants that is known to curing specialists in the
region and has been transmitted from one generation to the next since the
colonial period. For the purposes of my research, this region not only includes
the northern half of the peninsula, centered on the state of Yucatan, but also
includes the adjoining states of Campeche and Quintana Roo.

Collecting plants with traditional healers provided me with unusual
opportunities to become acquainted with them on a personal level. Contrary
to popular notions and scholarly writing on the subject, I found that the traditional healers are quite open in regard to their treatments, practices, and life
experiences. Their willingness to share this information with a stranger made
this book possible. The curers share a number of personal attributes: natural
curiosity, the desire to help others, patience, a good memory, a measure of
independence, and religious conviction.

None of the curers I have come to know has become wealthy or famous
from their skills. Although the role of the curer may once have been prestigious,
this is no longer the case. The attitudes expressed by laymen and the self-
perceptions of the curers suggest a high degree of ambiguity concerning the
role of the traditional healer. Their medical skills may be acknowledged by
some local people, but they are disparaged by others as rustics. Curers may

be suspected of witchcraft and are often vilified by evangelical groups (and some Catholics). Curing in Yucatan is at once deeply spiritual and empirically oriented, addressing problems of the body, spirit, and mind.

In exploring the ways in which curers learn their craft, two basic patterns have emerged: curers either learn voluntarily from elders or they are recruited through revelatory dreams. The men who learned their skills through dreams also established a connection to supernatural beings called *Balams*. These supernaturals communicate with curers through the medium of the *sastuns* (divining stones or crystals) that are their gifts. *Sastuns* and their multiple uses are discussed in depth in chapters 4 and 5.

My data on curing specialties, or components of curing practices, mirror those recorded in various ethnographic studies of the area undertaken with the support of the Carnegie Institute in the 1930s and 1940s (Redfield 1941; Redfield and Villa Rojas 1934; Steggerda 1941, 1943). The works of Mary Elmendorf (1976) and Rosita Arvigo (1994) provide more recent points of comparison. Although curers tended to describe an idealized model with different specialists treating different ailments, the reality I encountered was a different matter. There is a tremendous amount of overlap. Individual practices freely combine a number of different components, such as prayer, massage, plant medicine, magical practices, and Western medicine. Plant medicine is the common denominator; however, there is no distinction made between it and plant magic, or between empirical and magical treatments. The curer may act as a doctor, priest, witch, and psychiatrist.

It is difficult to contemplate common treatments without addressing traditional concepts of disease and its cause. The diagnosis and treatment of "culture-bound" diseases such as evil eye, evil winds, *bilis,* and *pasmo* are discussed in chapter 6. I hypothesize that an ideal of mental, physical, and spiritual balance underlies the conceptions of these illnesses and guides their treatment. Imbalances may be rectified by ritual actions or a variety of therapies.

The relationship between the present-day plant names and plant uses I recorded and those found in colonial-period sources demonstrates that the same set of plants has been utilized for at least several centuries by those with specialized knowledge of the local flora. The survival of traditional Yucatecan plant use may be due to the seemingly contradictory cultural conservatism and flexibility of its practitioners. The curers manage simultaneously to maintain their traditions, while incorporating new treatments, practices, and ideas into them. Contemporary Yucatecan curing reflects a unified regional oral tradition that continues to evolve with the passing of time. The past remains closely connected to the present in Yucatan, and my research into the present-day situation of curers and curing provided me with an intriguing backward glimpse into that past.

The Setting

Had the decision been mine to make, I probably would not have chosen Pisté as my research base. In some respects the town is marginal to both the modern and the traditional worlds of Yucatan. The proximity to the ruins of Chichén Itzá, one of the most visited archaeological sites in Mexico, has been mentioned. Tourists arrive daily in buses and rental cars. However, few of them come to Pisté itself, except to look for cheaper lodgings or food, which may be found on the main road, along with a liquor store that serves as the unofficial bank for the local populace and the tourists, a pharmacy, a post office, and a new public telephone station.

Many roads and paths lead from the scruffy main road into more rural neighborhoods. The houses along the main road and surrounding the plaza are mostly squat concrete structures. The farther one gets from this central zone, the more likely it is for such houses to be replaced by those of the traditional, thatched variety. The poorer of the traditional houses have walls of poles, whereas the more prosperous dwellings have concrete or stacked stone bases.

Much of the population still supports itself to some extent by farming. Pisté is located in the breadbasket, or more accurately, the corn belt, of the peninsula. The majority of older women wear traditional clothing, but many younger women do not. Very few people have European features; many could have served as models for Classic-era sculptors. The present population of Pisté is about 3,500.

The ruins provide service jobs for some of the townspeople, along with a first-hand look at the material culture of wealthy visitors. Televisions are not uncommon. They bring soap operas from Miami into homes and businesses, portraying lifestyles and selling products that are equally seductive and unattainable for most of Pisté's viewers. Many objects I consider mundane, such as metal cooking utensils, must be purchased in Valladolid or Mérida. Beef is available in the small meat market twice a week. School supplies, such as pencils, are scarce and expensive. There are so many children in town that the school maintains a schedule of two shifts per day. A government clinic in Valladolid provides free medical care, but often local people cannot afford to fill the prescriptions they receive there. A satellite clinic in town seems to be open rarely.

Chichén Itzá's massive ruins serve as an inescapable reminder of a vanished past, and people in Pisté are proud of their ancestors. Unexcavated structures and pottery shards appear unexpectedly in the surrounding fields and woods. The old church in the main plaza, whose lintel bears the date 1734, contains ancient carved blocks of stone from pre-Hispanic times and sits across an expanse of concrete from the new, generic concrete church. Everybody loves the new church because it is bigger, although it cannot accommodate all who wish to attend on important holy days. As in all Mexican towns, the plaza is a gathering place for young and old alike. It is the setting for traditional dances and rituals, which, although unknown in Rome, are seamlessly linked to the Catholic calendar and the activities of the church in Pisté.

The people of Pisté live between the Maya past and the national Mexican present: culturally, symbolically, and geographically. A new highway, a very expensive toll road, passes within a few kilometers of the town, enabling tourists to travel between the capital city of Mérida in the northwestern corner of the peninsula and the sprawling resort of Cancún in the northeast without having to slow down for the countless intervening small towns on the old road. Many younger people commute to jobs in Cancún, traveling the old road in second-class buses. They return to Pisté, and the more traditional lifestyle it offers, on weekends.

My chance meeting with one of these commuters led me to Pisté. Don Tomás, my first Maya friend, works as a custodian of a small Postclassic site in Quintana Roo, but his home is in Pisté. I came to the town after Don Tomás invited me to visit there and learn more about plants. The invitation was made after my first research trip to the state of Quintana Roo to study Yucatecan plant uses with him. At first I found it odd that this very modern commuting trend played such a vital part in my introduction to traditional medicine in Yucatan, but an analogy can be drawn: commuting allows a modified version of traditional life to continue in the small towns and villages of Yucatan, just as the incorporation of nontraditional elements has contributed to the survival of traditional medicine in places like Pisté. In time, Pisté has become beautiful to me.

A Methodological Note

I have established a good working relationship with several traditional healers living in and around Pisté and have conducted six brief research trips there to record information about the ways in which they use local plants. I have changed the names of the curers who made this book possible. Each trip lasted one month or less. I interviewed the curers and recorded information about each plant that was shown to me, including applicable plant names in Maya and Spanish, a description of its habit and blooming season, and its uses, including the method of use and the quantities used in prescriptions. Translations of the interviews are my own (as are all errors in translation). Too few studies include information on how to use a plant for a given complaint. Several curers have suggested to me that a compendium of this information would be of interest to many Yucatecans as a practical guide to self-care. These data appear in appendix A. I collected voucher specimens according to standard herbarium practices, and my collection (178 numbers) is on deposit at Tulane University's Herbarium. To date, I have executed field sketches of about half of the collection, as the flora of Yucatan has not been thoroughly surveyed and has rarely been illustrated. Thirty-six botanical illustrations are included here. The illustrations are arranged alphabetically according to scientific binomial.

CHAPTER TWO
The Yucatecan Sources

Ethnobotany is by nature an interdisciplinary field, and several different kinds of sources provide a context for my research. The sources include ethnographies and ethnohistorical works, as well as ethnobotanical and botanical studies. I have been very fortunate to have at my disposal a number of ethnographic works written about Yucatecan towns that are geographically and culturally close to my research base in Pisté. These works have provided me with a relatively recent reference point for studying traditional plant use in the area.

Robert Redfield and Alfonso Villa Rojas' (1962) work, *Chan Kom: A Maya Village,* is a thorough account of the "mode of life" of a peasant village located some fifteen kilometers from Pisté. The Chan Kom study was one component of a larger research design undertaken by the Carnegie Institution of Washington, the goal of which was to explore ethnological and sociological topics in Yucatan. Chan Kom was selected as an example, or archetype, of a Yucatecan peasant village.

In 1941, Redfield published *Folk Culture of Yucatán,* which includes comparative material gathered in separate studies conducted in four communities on the peninsula: Tusik, Chan Kom, Dzitás, and Mérida. Redfield saw these communities as points lying along a continuum from folk to urban societies. Tusik, an isolated village in Quintana Roo state, was seen as the most culturally homogeneous community, whereas the capital city, Mérida, was the least homogeneous, or most "disorganized," society of the four studied. Chan Kom and Dzitás were the intermediate points. Dzitás, as a larger town located along a railroad line by which influences from the capital arrived, had a society that was more urban, individualized, and secularized than that of Chan Kom. Chan Kom was at that time linked to the main road that passes by the ruins of Chichén Itzá (about two kilometers from Pisté), but only by a rough, unpaved road.

As Irwin Press (1975:12) pointed out in the introduction to his monograph on the town of Pustunich in the Puuc zone of Yucatan, *Tradition and Adaptation: Life in a Modern Yucatan Maya Village,* Chan Kom was a somewhat atypical community in that it had been founded not so many years before the arrival of Redfield and Villa Rojas, and its population was composed of refugees from older villages destroyed during the Caste War.

The same could be said of Pisté, a fact that makes the similarities between the information recorded by Redfield and Villa Rojas on Chan Kom and my information from Pisté all the more striking. The presence of Americans and other foreigners nearby at Chichén Itzá has also been a factor influencing both communities, perhaps making them even less perfect examples of Redfield's elusive archetypal village. Chan Kom has subsequently been studied to an unusual degree; it is the subject of Redfield's (1950) follow-up study, *A Village that Chose Progress: Chan Kom Revisited,* and the site of Mary Elmendorf's research on the role of peasant women in Yucatec society, which resulted in the publication of *Nine Mayan Women* (Elmendorf 1976).

Theoretical criticisms aside, the broad scope and thorough scholarship of *Chan Kom: A Maya Village* make it a most important resource for me, providing a "snap-shot" of Pisté's neighbors as they lived sixty-two years ago. Redfield and Villa Rojas' information concerning the division of labor, agricultural rituals and ceremonies, and the medicine of the village have been particularly helpful. Their study provided me with the linguistic leads that guided my insight into the range of curing specialties and specialists practicing in and around Pisté.

At times, the "ethnographic present" described in *Chan Kom* seems enviably rich in Maya traditions compared to the data I recorded in Pisté, although I subscribe to Press' theory that Yucatecan society is capable of adjusting to change and progress and will continue to retain traditional elements that contribute to modern life.

Redfield's (1941) analysis of similarities and differences among the communities of Tusik, Chan Kom, Dzitás, and Mérida in *The Folk Culture of Yucatan* gives a broader perspective on the traditions of the peninsula and an understanding of its different zones. The chapters concerning the decline of the Maya gods and interrelationships between medicine and magic were most helpful to this research. Villa Rojas' fieldwork in Tusik, synthesized by Redfield in *The Folk Culture of Yucatan,* is also the basis of his later monograph, *The Maya of East Central Quintana Roo* (Villa Rojas 1945), which concerns the village of Tusik and the Santa Cruz Maya subtribe of X-Cacal.

Morris Steggerda, another Carnegie Institution scholar, worked in northeastern Yucatan at roughly the same time as Redfield and Villa Rojas. His original research interest was in the anthropometry of the Yucatecan Maya, but he subsequently published *Maya Indians of Yucatan,* an ethnography of the town of Pisté. Pisté was selected because of its proximity to the Carnegie Institution's facilities at Chichén Itzá. The historical background and demographics of the town are useful to understanding the social context of Pisté. Steggerda's description of the seasonal round of *milpa* (slash-and-burn agricultural field used for growing corn, beans, and other crops) farming, which remains the economic backbone of the community, provides an ecological context. He also includes data concerning nonutilitarian plant use and conceptions of disease.

Originally written as one of six appendices to *Maya Indians of Yucatan*, Steggerda published "Some Ethnological Data Concerning One Hundred Yucatecan Plants" in 1943. That study was based on a collection of voucher specimens made primarily in Pisté. His concern is botanical, rather than cultural, and he writes rather disparagingly about traditional medicine.

Robert Redfield's wife, Margaret Park Redfield, accompanied Redfield to Yucatan. During her stay in the town of Dzitás, she and her husband collaborated on a monograph called *Disease and its Cure in Dzitás* (Redfield and Redfield 1940), which includes case histories tracing the course of several incidents of disease through the stages of diagnosis, treatment, and resolution. This brief volume describes the practices of several curers in Dzitás and their clientele.

Elmendorf's (1976) work, *Nine Mayan Women*, attempts an in-depth look at the lives of a small number of Maya women through vignettes based upon interviews and personal interpretations of the women's interrelationships. Elmendorf's research was guided by Redfield's theoretical framework. Progress is seen as an inevitable process that offers the women new possibilities at the same time as it erodes traditional society. The author mentions that she chose Chan Kom for her study, after speaking with Villa Rojas, in order to add a feminine dimension to previous anthropological studies of the village. Although the interviews are rather impressionistic, they provide glimpses of the worldview and personal expectations of the women of Chan Kom. One key woman, Luz, is a curer, but Elmendorf does not fully explore her role as such. Elmendorf's humanistic approach and inclusion of interview materials were helpful to the preparation of my own research.

Rosita Arvigo's (1994) book, *Sastun,* is more an autobiography than an ethnography, and it is set in Belize rather than in Yucatan. However, *Sastun* recounts the author's personal experiences as an apprentice to a traditional Maya curer, and as such it provides a valuable point of comparison on several levels. Arvigo obviously loves and respects Don Eligio Pantí, the curer to whom she becomes apprenticed, and her writing about him is refreshing after reading impersonal accounts of what curers do. Arvigo's attitude toward traditional medicine is worlds away from that of Morris Steggerda; she is somewhat mystical but also has a pragmatic approach toward medicinal plants as effective therapies, and she also explores ways in which the renewable resources of the rainforest may be salvaged.

One more ethnography, set even farther afield in a small town near San Luis Potosí, also influenced my work. Ruth Behar's (1993) *Translated Woman* is a detailed life history of one woman, Esperanza. It is also a meditation upon the difficulties of understanding and writing about someone from another culture in a way that does not reduce them to a caricature of themselves. The author reflects on the inequalities between her own life and that of Esperanza, which allow her the luxury of "translating" another person's life. In this sense, the book is a double portrait of the author and the woman whose life history she writes. Behar's excellent book addresses many of the concerns I had during the course of my fieldwork and succeeds in allowing the voice of her subject to speak for herself.

Yucatan is a unique place, geographically and culturally apart from the rest of Mexico. Information concerning Yucatecan plants and their uses differs from information about the ethnoflora of other parts of Mexico in terms of both quantity and quality. Perhaps because the Spanish conquest went on for so long in Yucatan, there are few early Spanish colonial works on local plants and their uses compared to existing sources from central Mexico.

From the first days of the colonial era, Spanish writers were fascinated by the advanced medical knowledge of the Aztecs. Books 10 and 11 of Fray Bernardino de Sahagún's (1975) famous *General History of the Things of New Spain* is a compilation of medical information described by local doctors and contains many illustrations of plants. Many scholars consider Sahagún to be the first ethnographer in New Spain.

The Badianus manuscript, or *Libellus de Medicinalibus Indorum Herbis* (Emmart 1940; Guerra 1952), is another early colonial-period medical work with botanical illustrations. It was probably written and illustrated by native doctors at the College of Tlatelolco. This hypothesis is borne out by the style of the illustrations, which incorporate Aztec pictographs and so provide visual information about the habitat of the plants described.

King Phillip the Second dispatched Francisco Hernández, a Spanish physician, to Mexico specifically to write about the natural history of the country. Hernández' *Rerum Medicarum Nova Hispania Thesaurus* (Hernández 1959) was the result of this assignment.

There are no comparable works from Yucatan. Bishop Diego de Landa's encyclopedic *Relación de las cosas de Yucatán* (Landa 1941) contains information about curers and plants but strangely contains no plant illustrations. One edition of Landa's (1938) *Relación de las cosas de Yucatán* includes an appendix with ten *relaciones* written by *encomenderos* of Yucatan between the years 1579–85, and contains plant descriptions.

There are, however, a number of extant Maya texts that contain information about local plants and their uses. The Chilam Balam books, named for towns in which they were found, deal with a range of subjects: medicine, astronomy, calendrics, and history. The Ixil (Latin American Library at Tulane University, Ixil, Chilam Balam de. Ms.), Kaua (Latin American Library at

Tulane University, Kaua, Chilam Balam de. Ms.), Tekax, and Nah (*Manuscritos de Tekax y Nah* 1981) are the most medically oriented of these.[1] The town of Kaua is located only forty kilometers east of Pisté. During the course of my research I was able to compare Maya plant names and plant uses recorded in the Kaua manuscript to those in my collection. I have been able to do so thanks to Dr. Victoria Bricker, who has generously allowed me to work with then unpublished translation of the second volume of the manuscript.

The late-colonial Mena and Sotuta manuscripts (Latin American Library at Tulane University, Mena Ms. and Sotuta Ms.) are written in Maya and are purely medical in content. They contain medical prescriptions for a variety of illnesses. Both works were translated by Ralph Roys, and copies of his translations are in the Latin American Library of Tulane University.

Yerbas y hechicerías del Yucatán (Latin American Library at Tulane University) is another colonial-period manuscript in Tulane University's Latin American Library. It is most probably the work of an Italian physician, Ricardo Ossado, alias *"el Judio"* (The Jew), who lived and worked in Valladolid in the middle of the eighteenth century. Ossado wrote about local plants and their uses, recording most plant names in Maya.

Yerbas y hechicerías, the Chilam Balam books, and the Maya medical works may all be seen as compendiums or editions of earlier information. *Yerbas y hechicerías* seems to have been the basis for a whole complex of later books on the subject of Yucatecan medicine and plant use, including Benjamin Cuevas' (1913) *Plantas medicinales de Yucatán y guía médica práctica doméstica* and Joaquín and Juan Dondé's (1907) *Apuntes sobre las plantas de Yucatán.* The most recent work relating to *Yerbas y hechicerías* is Maximino Martínez' (1933) *Las plantas medicinales de México.* This work is composed of four separate parts. The first section of the book deals with scientifically identified plants whose properties have been tested, the second deals with scientifically identified plants with untested properties, the third contains unidentified plants, and the fourth is a version of Ossado's work.

Ralph Roys' (1931) work, *The Ethno-Botany of the Maya,* is a compilation of colonial Maya and Spanish works, including the Mena and Sotuta manuscripts (Latin American Library at Tulane University, Mena Ms. and Sotuta Ms.), as well as the Chilam Balam books from Ixil (Latin American Library at Tulane University, Ixil, Chilam Balam de. Ms.), Tekax, Nah (*Manuscritos de*

---

1. For a discussion of the Chilam Balam books as a group see Edmonson and Bricker's (1985) "Yucatecan Literature" in the *Supplement to the Handbook of Middle American Indians* and Barrera Vásquez and Rendón's (1948) *El libro de los libros de Chilam Balam.*

Tekax y Nah 1981), and the first part of the Kaua manuscript (Latin American Library at Tulane University, Kaua, Chilam Balam de. Ms.). Roys asked his colleague, the famous botanist Paul Standley, to identify the plants mentioned in the colonial manuscripts. Steggerda's (1943) study, "Some Ethnological Data Concerning One Hundred Yucatecan Plants," compares twentieth-century plant uses to those in Roys' *The Ethno-Botany of the Maya,* and so initiated a research strategy that I have continued here.

Standley's work on the flora of Mexico includes *Trees and Shrubs of Mexico* (1920–26) and *Flora of Yucatan* (1930). The last-mentioned book was the result of Standley's reorganization of a number of different early collections of Yucatecan flora, including the specimens of Millspaugh, Gaumer, Valdez, and Greenman.

Rosa Mendieta and Silvia del Amo's (1981) *Plantas medicinales del estado de Yucatán* is a catalog of regional flora. The plants mentioned are those that appear in a number of different sources, including Martínez (1933), *Yerbas y hechicerías* (ca. 1750), Roys (1931), and Standley (1930). The catalog provides common names and uses for the plants and is arranged according to scientific name. It also has some illustrations.

Beatrice Roeder's (1988) work, *Chicano Folk Medicine from Los Angeles,* is oriented toward improving the medical care of that city's Hispanic population by examining culturally salient beliefs concerning illness and disease causation. Interviews with Mexican Americans reveal the use of plants as both medicine and preventive agents. An excellent appendix provides historical and modern information on medicinals.

Finally, Dennis Breedlove and Robert Laughlin's (1993) work, *The Flowering of Man: A Tzotzil Botany of Zinacantán,* expands the field of ethnobotany to include cultural materials such as stories and poems that demonstrate the range of human-plant interaction in this highland community. The book contains excellent botanical illustrations, as well as drawings of articles of Zinacantán's material culture.

In general, the focus of these sources is on the plants rather than on the curers. I hope that the present work will expand that focus to include the people who continue the oral traditions of Yucatecan curing and who know the most about the medicinal and useful plants in their environment. Examined as a whole, the manuscripts and books discussed here demonstrate a sustained interest in the plants of the peninsula since the beginning of the colonial period and the renewal of that interest today.

CHAPTER THREE

Portraits of the Curers

I thought it would be easy to write about the curers of Yucatan, some of whom I have known and worked with for a period of five years. This group of individuals welcomed me into their culture, lives, and in some cases, into their families. They have trusted me to "do it right" with this "book" about traditional curing in Yucatan and a few of the people who practice it, and I have struggled with the burden of this honor. Although a comparatively large amount of data has been compiled describing the behavior of Maya curers within ritual contexts in various parts of the Maya world, very little has been written about the curers themselves. Was there any common thread, some shared personality traits or life experiences that tied these individuals to each other? Or set them apart from the other members of their society? Perhaps the most interesting aspect of my research experience has been the nonissue of my entrance into friendships with these traditional practitioners.

Throughout the course of this research, I have continued to reflect on just why I have been accepted into what has been generally thought of as exclusive or restricted cultural territory. I feel both fortunate and grateful, although I cannot say exactly why I have been allowed into this garden. Maya friends shrug and say it was my destiny to come to them in Yucatan. Perhaps it had something to do with my being an artist. People in Yucatan seemed to respect this skill and instantly related to and approved of my plan to use it to illustrate "their" plants. But having been the recipient of so much hospitality over the years, I am more inclined to say that the larger answer more likely lies within the collective "personality" or "temperament" of Yucatecan Maya people themselves, rather than with me. I believe that the people I have gotten to know would have been as accepting and generous with anyone who approached them with a genuine interest in their culture, a bit of language skill, and a nonaggressive attitude.

One could interject into this Apollonian interpretation that associating with a rich foreigner would probably be seen by those within the society as an opportunity for potential rewards in terms of both status and money. This is undeniably true, although I believe that they were supplementary, rather than primary, reasons for my acceptance. Whatever the reasons, I have gained as much emotionally as intellectually from the experience. In *Translated Woman*, Behar (1993:271) pointed out that "any ethnographic representation . . . includes a self-representation." I would add that this activity also implies a self-examination.

The experience of reading *Translated Woman* was an epiphany for me for several reasons. I knew many things that I did not want my work to be modeled after, pitfalls that I wanted to avoid, but this was a long way from having a positive course plotted for my research. I was encouraged to read something where I felt that the author had sensitively examined and grappled with many of the same issues that have intrigued me during the course of my research. Specifically, Behar's work addressed the ways in which issues of class and race can intercept cross-cultural understanding and also the position of privilege from which writers of ethnographies/life histories speak. Although not rich by the standards of my own country, I struggled with the role of Rich Gringa Student in which I found myself cast over and over in Yucatan. I was uncomfortable but fully aware that the research presented here began serendipitously precisely because I had had the luxury of taking a vacation to snorkel and dive in the warm waters of the Caribbean. Just how unimaginable these circumstances were to most Yucatecan Mayas became as clear and crystalline as the sea I had come to visit.

I hope that this book, which is the result of an interdisciplinary graduate experience, will reflect the various methods and techniques of both the sciences and the humanities, from which I have drawn freely during the course of the field research and have hoped to integrate herein. It is easier to deal empirically with plants than people. These "portraits," then, will be the most narrative section of this work. While writing them, the sensation of being a betrayer of confidences, an abuser of friendships, has descended upon me at intervals. I try to balance my guilt with the positive hope expressed by many of the following people that it would be good for non-Mayas to know more about Maya curing and the people who do it. I hope to live up to their expectations of me. And I hope that their voices, although "translated" across borders of both language and culture, will be audible throughout this work over the "interference" of the author's voice. I will have the responsibility of (re)translating these words when reading this to the people portrayed here.

Don Tomás

Don Tomás was my first Maya friend. I met him the summer before I started graduate school at his place of work, a small, leafy, Postclassic archaeological site in Quintana Roo state filled with crumbly ruins and birdsong where he works for Instituto Nacional de Antropología e Historia (INAH) as a *guardian* (custodian). He is an unusually open person (by the standards of any culture that I can imagine), and I owe my subsequent entry into the world of curing in Yucatan, and indeed into the Maya world, to him.

During that first visit, as he showed my husband and me around the archaeo-logical site the day after a tropical storm, Don Tomás rattled off information on seemingly every plant we passed. He must have approved of my interest, because at the end of the day he invited me to return to learn more about plants from him. My mind had caught fire, with Don Tomás' knowledge of local plants and the sight of a charred bundle left in a tree (an offering to the spirits of the wild game animals left by some hopeful hunter) making me feel a living connection to traditional ways about which I knew nothing. I only knew that I had to learn more about them.

Whether Don Tomás really thought I would come back or not I do not know. He never received the letter announcing my impending arrival during the following summer (of 1991). I remember standing alone in the middle of the plants he was watering on the first day of that second trip, foolishly reading aloud a copy of the missing letter stating my earnest desire to take him up on his most gracious offer to teach me and hoping that he had meant it after all and had not changed his mind.

Don Tomás did not initially seem to remember me until I identified myself as the gringa who had showed up after the *chubasco* Diana (tropical rainstorm Diana). I knew that I felt and looked ridiculous standing there reading from my letter, but he did not laugh. My lessons about the plants of Yucatan started that day. He did not want to accept the small salary that my advisors had suggested would be appropriate. By the end of this trip, Don Tomás had invited me to visit "next time" at his village, Pisté, in Yucatan state, so that I could meet other, older people who, he insisted, knew more about traditional plant use than he did. Over the next few visits Don Tomás introduced me to other curers, and Pisté became the main site for my research.

So, how to describe this most important gatekeeper? Don Tomás is in his early forties, is rather short by Maya standards (*un chaparrito* [a person short in stature, "runt"]), and is almost always smiling. He is straightforward and patient and has always been willing to try to answer my most difficult or ignorant questions on the most arcane subjects. His attitude that "one learns by asking questions" made me feel more comfortable about always asking him endless (and sometimes foolishly repetitive) questions. He has always taken me and my research seriously, but this is not to say that anyone is exempt from Don Tomás' sense of humor.

Don Tomás comes from a long line of curers, or better said, of *h-mens* (Maya curers or shamans). One reason he has put up with me and my questions is that he hopes that our working together will result in making the accomplishments and skills of the Mayas of Yucatan better known to a wider world. I have not deluded him about my doubts about my ability to do so, nor about my own rather marginal position in that world. Notwithstanding, Don Tomás has been both ambassador for his culture and friend during the course of my subsequent trips to Yucatan. This research would not have occurred without him. He has not only introduced us to his world, but welcomed my husband and me into his family.

There is an especially close tie between Don Tomás and his wife, Mariela, and my husband, Kim, and me. We are age-mates in his large extended family, of which we have essentially become fictive kin. If we could have arranged to be in Yucatan for the baptism of Don Tomás and Mariela's daughter, Marina, I suspect that this link would have been made official by our becoming godparents to the baby. It is with Mariela that I correspond, sending news about our families back and forth across the Gulf of Mexico.

Don Tomás and Mariela also have a son, Juan, who is now a shy but curious teenager who enjoys accompanying his father to the *milpa* and on plant-hunting expeditions. Don Tomás travels back and forth between Pisté and his job in the state of Quintana Roo and so is only able to spend weekends at home with his family. Don Tomás and Mariela's marriage is strong despite this stressful, but not very unusual, arrangement. Indeed, their affectionate relationship, characterized by much joking banter, is perhaps far more unusual than the schedule on which it exists, as many Yucatecans (not just men) find themselves commuting between jobs (often in cities) and home villages.

Perhaps it is unfair to begin Don Tomás' *historia* ("history," "tale," or "story") with a description of my relationship to him, but he is the inspiration and starting point for this work. The story of our meeting is the framing device, à la Scheherazade, that describes the context in which I began this research. It seems logical to my linear Western mind to proceed chronologically. In this way, I will also be writing about the people I have spent the most time with, and know best, first.

Don Tomás might not even call himself a curer, because he treats only members of his own family and friends (and is very modest), but he is extremely knowledgeable about plant medicine, different curing techniques, and Yucatecan agricultural rituals. He dreams of visiting and learning from different curers of the peninsula after his retirement in another fifteen years. Whether this would be for purely personal enrichment or perhaps professional study I am not sure, but his interest in the just-named topics has been lifelong.

Don Tomás was born on a *rancho* (isolated homestead) eight kilometers from Old Chichén Itzá. His family spoke Maya at home, and he learned Spanish when he attended grammar school in the village of Pisté (about a twenty-two-kilometer round-trip journey). Don Tomás stressed the practical advantages of attempting to learn medical skills while living on a *rancho,* but his natural inclination toward the subject also played a part in his decision. Don Tomás, like his mother and father, may have learned about curing out of necessity, but they could also draw on the experience of family members, particularly on his mother's side.

Don Tomás' paternal uncle was a curer, as were his grandfather and great-grandfather on his mother's side. The last-named personage was the rebel Maya leader, Jacinto Pat, who fought to drive out the whites from Yucatan during the Caste War of the late nineteenth century. Although I was familiar with his name from accounts of the Caste War (see, for example, Nelson Reed's [1964] *The Caste War in Yucatán* for a historical account and Allan F. Burns' [1983] *An Epoch of Miracles: Oral Literature of the Yucatec Maya,* for narratives that mention Jacinto Pat's exploits), I was surprised to hear that this well-known warrior was also a curer. Don Tomás said that he had been a curer in the town of Tihosuco, who later moved east and settled near Chichén Itzá. Don Tomás describes his grandfather, another curer, as having been a *teniente* (lieutenant) in the Caste War. This grandfather "knew the work of the masseur, also of the bone setter, and lastly of plants."

Don Tomás gradually learned how to use plants as he accompanied his father, uncle, and grandfather to the *milpa* and the forest to do their daily work. He still knows the trails and paths of Xtojil "like the palm of my hand."

As a child, Don Tomás took part in numerous Maya ceremonies, including the *ch'a chaac* (rainmaking ceremony). He told me about his participation in five *ch'a chaac* ceremonies, which were presided over by a *h-men* named Justo from Ticimul, a place about ten kilometers distant from Xtojil. To help attract the rain, he and other little boys sat under a table of specially prepared offerings and played the part of frogs: "Cleck clock uo, uo, that's how we'd sing, all alike. There was a man who told us when to sing during the ceremony." Don Tomás says that the rain always began the same day the ceremonies were completed, after the *h-men* had returned to his home village.

Don Tomás proudly describes his uncle, grandfather, and great-grandfather as *h-mens:* "They each had their *sastuns;* their powers were strong." This was one of the very few times during the course of this research that anyone has openly applied the term *h-men* to themselves or to a relative, which speaks to both Don Tomás' pride in his heritage and his characteristic openness to me. Others repeatedly rejected labeling themselves as *yerbateros* (herbalists) or *h-mens,* a reticence that may stem from a fear of being suspected of witchcraft by neighbors, a sense of modesty, or because people feel that such a statement is tantamount to admitting to being somewhat rustic. In the past, being a *h-men* or a *yerbatero* was probably a status-enhancing occupation; perceptions have shifted in this regard.

As part of his training with INAH, Don Tomás has traveled extensively within the Republic. Of the curers in this book, he is the most fully integrated into Mexico's national society and the most knowledgeable in the ways of the non-Maya world. Perhaps this is simply because Don Tomás is the youngest of the curers I have come to know and so reflects the social changes and wider opportunities now available in Yucatan.

Don Tomás' work as a custodian for INAH also puts him in contact with tourists and occasionally with scholars from many countries. He has begun studying English in order to communicate better with these visitors. Don Tomás keeps up with world news by reading the newspaper and has often stumped me with questions about such topics as the structure of state- and national-level government in the United States, or the functions of our healthcare and legal systems. He is very curious about the United States and how it functions. Don Tomás' goodwill and enthusiasm for this project has kept it and my hopes for its eventual completion alive.

Don Pedro

The first "person who knows plants" to whom Don Tomás introduced me in Pisté was his father-in-law, Don Pedro. Although I now enjoy a close relationship with Don Pedro, this friendship did not come about in an effortless manner. Don Pedro is in his early sixties but looks younger. He is tall and strong, with a face that often looks severe, even when relaxed. He looks the part he plays of paterfamilias to his large extended family. He and his wife, Doña Luz, have six children. Of these six (four daughters and two sons), the families of all but one son live within the family compound that takes up almost an entire block near the town's central plaza. The eldest son, named after his father, makes his home away from the family compound but within the village of Pisté.

Don Pedro makes *milpa* for the entire family, with the occasional assistance of Don Tomás. He works alone in the fields much of the time, which is somewhat unusual, especially for someone his age. Men are often assisted in their labors in the fields by their brothers, sons, or their sons-in-law. In many ways, Don Pedro strikes me as being the family's keeper of the old ways. Doña Luz is very much co-anchor of this tightly-bound family, but her domain is that of the household and Catholicism, whereas it is Don Pedro who cleaves to the traditional lifestyle of making *milpa* and keeps alive the Maya stories of *uayoob* (transforming witches), *aluxes* (small beings who have the form of men and can be mischievous if not propitiated with gifts of food), and lore of the fields.

Like his son-in-law, Don Pedro has had many experiences with foreigners. His father came to Pisté from the town of Oxkutzcab in the southwestern part of the peninsula in order to work as a laborer in the ruins of Chichén Itzá. Pisté's history has been linked to that of the ruins for some time. The town has supplied laborers for archaeological investigations there from at least the time of the Carnegie Institute's studies in the 1930s. Nowadays, Pisté provides tourist services to visitors of the ruins.

In his younger days, Don Pedro worked with several archaeologists, including E. Wyllys Andrews IV, at Maya sites including Chichén Itzá and Dzibilchaltún (near Mérida). He remembers the archaeologists as being good to work for and very generous (overly so, in his opinion) with alcohol. Living and working with the archaeological crews for several months at a time opened up new vistas for Don Pedro, and he seems to have enjoyed working with these various expeditions.

I wonder if Don Pedro would say the same about the seasonal work in several service positions he has held at the elegant hotels that fringe the archaeological zone of Chichén Itzá. He has worked as a bartender, porter, and room-cleaner, balancing this work with the yearly schedule of burning, planting, and tending his fields. Over the years, he has made many friends of different nationalities. The contacts with foreign visitors have not all been positive. As we got to know each other a little better, and he learned that I, too, had worked as a bartender in the restaurant business for many years, Don Pedro regaled me with horrific tales of the behavior and attitudes of some of the tourists he has known and then swore me to secrecy about them. The ignorance and prejudice on the part of some wealthy visitors is difficult for such a dignified person to shrug off or tolerate. I had to earn Don Pedro's trust gradually, over time. At the beginning of our friendship, he was distantly cordial, treating me much as he would probably treat any gringa who walked into his bar.

We met on New Year's Eve. I decided to take up Don Tomás on his offer to visit Pisté. My husband and I were expected, but when we asked where Don Tomás' house was, as per our instructions, no one was willing to tell us. Finally, someone (who turned out to be the tenant in a rental property belonging to some family member of Don Tomás) asked us to wait while he "went to look" for Don Tomás.

Don Tomás and his son appeared on a bicycle a little while later and invited us to join them for dinner at Don Pedro and Doña Luz' house. We had no idea that New Year's Eve is a very family-centered holiday in Mexico. Kim (my husband) and I were swept along on a wave of Don Tomás' hospitality right into a slightly awkward experience at his in-laws' family compound. All the children and their families, as well as several visiting relatives, were congregated in the dining room. Don Pedro was seated at the head of the table, and I remember being seated next to him. It was a gala dinner, with everyone dressed in their finest clothes. I felt I could hear Don Pedro wondering why his son-in-law had to go and invite strangers, and gringos at that, to an important family celebration. But he was incredibly polite and made a point of telling me about things Maya. Like Don Tomás, Don Pedro is obviously proud of his cultural heritage. I knew that I wanted his wife, Doña Luz, to be my adopted mother after that night. She radiated a calm pride in her family and a gentle curiosity that contrasted with Don Pedro's hauteur. The meal went on forever, or perhaps it only seemed that way because it was my first experience of eating while so many pairs of eyes observed the manner in which I did so.

Later during that same visit, Don Pedro expressed his willingness to work with me, to teach me about local plants and their uses. He said that he would do so because I "didn't push." Many things Don Pedro taught me were "only for my knowledge," which makes this portrait more difficult to write. I feel ethically obligated to omit interesting topics, but so be it. It was a bumpy road for both of us to reach the present stage of our relationship, where I have become an adopted daughter in the house of Don Pedro and Doña Luz, and I will not violate that trust.

Don Pedro grew up not far from Pisté, in the nearby community of Chicimul. He says that he began learning about plant medicine from his father when he was about twelve years old, when he accompanied him to the family's *milpa*. Unlike his father, Don Pedro employs massage as a component of his curing repertoire. He taught himself how to relieve the pain he sometimes felt in his hands or bones. As he puts it,

> I would work the tendons, I had to do it . . . this is what you can do—because when one has injured a tendon, you just grab it like this, and you feel where it's moving and that is where it is affected. One goes on working it, in whatever part of the body.

Don Pedro, like Don Tomás, cures only family and friends. Neither he nor his father used the *sastuns* or conducted the agricultural rituals (such as the ritual of first harvest, rainmaking, and so forth) that define the role of *h-men*. An analysis of that role will be covered in the next three chapters. Although the majority of Don Pedro's treatments are empirically oriented, I have recorded magical treatments and uses of plants working with him, and he has performed *limpios* (cleansing ceremonies) on me, my husband, and others to *quitar mal aire* (remove any evil winds that we might be carrying). Some of his treatments utilize plants to remove what I would term evil spells. Of course, this raises the possibility (at least in the eyes of the townspeople) that a person with such knowledge also knows how to place spells on people. However, the ratio of empirical to magical treatments in Don Pedro's repertoire is about the same as that of the other curers I have worked with. More information on common methods and treatments will be found in chapter 6.

I remember that early in our relationship, before I began staying in "my room" at his house (the one with the pots of lard and the sewing machine that faces the street and the competing serenades of the next-door neighbor's rooster and his radio), Don Pedro and my husband (an amateur chiropractor) exchanged massages in our room at Don Estéban's *posada* (inn). Don Pedro kneaded my husband's back muscles vigorously, working down from his shoulders. Then he began on the willing patient's legs. Both men were at least half-drunk but were very intent on this exchange of techniques. They were clearly bonding. I declined a massage out of modesty. Afterward, we three went out for a snack. When Don Pedro left the table for a moment, a man at the next table leaned over and asked in a stage whisper if "we didn't know that he (Don Pedro) was a witch?" Gossip must have spread around town after I responded that I was learning about plants from him. I retreated to the room to sleep, leaving the men to drink on into the night. The next day I attended a special prayer Doña Luz and her daughters held for Don Pedro's soul in their bedroom at the family altar.

I have not seen Don Pedro drink to excess except on that night, although I have the impression that he may have done his share of drinking when he was younger. That night of the massages I met another side of the person who is the proud grandfather and head of the household, the one next to whom I sat during that first dinner.

Learning about plants from Don Pedro was always a very different experience from my lessons with Don Tomás. He demanded that I learn the names and uses of the plants promptly. After I asked the name of something too many times during a collecting trip, Don Pedro exploded, "If you keep asking me the names of the plants, I will be the one who learns them. . . . I will be the one to ask the questions" and then proceeded to ask me the names of every plant we passed for the rest of the day. He shamed me into memorizing the plant names. I did not want him to be sorry he decided to teach me. He was sometimes impatient with the care and time I took writing everything down. It must be because my mind was too weak to retain properly what he was telling me. I always knew when I was not up to par with Don Pedro, because at those times he would tell me a story about some gringos from the United States who had spent six months at Chichén Itzá and learned the Maya language "perfectly" during that time. *They* had learned each thing you told them the first time.

Although I might not have been an ideal student in Don Pedro's eyes, we eventually became friends. Maybe it was because I kept him company on his usually solitary treks through the woods or because I helped him pick beans and shuck dried corn. Even if I could never measure up to those visitors who learned Maya perfectly, I did keep trying. And his wife and daughter liked me. For whatever reason, he accepted me. Much of what Don Pedro has told me was prefaced by his statement that "this is for only you to know; it isn't for scientists up there." The message seemed to be that telling other people lessens the power of what one has learned or experienced. When I tape-recorded an interview with Don Pedro covering the same topics we had discussed freely many times before, I felt as though he was giving an interview to a stranger from a newspaper. He spoke in a general way about Maya medicine, Maya life, and artfully evaded any direct or personal questions.

Don Cósimo

Don Tomás, gatekeeper and friend, also introduced me to Don Cósimo during my first visit to Pisté. Don Cósimo is a friend of Don Tomás' father and is
probably in his middle seventies. He seems older because his hair is streaked
with gray and because he is physically frail. He has a hunched back and an
atrophied arm, from which dangles a hand injured by a machete in a long-
ago accident. Unlike Don Pedro, Don Cósimo's face has a gentle, almost soft
quality to it. When he smiles, he looks young. He initially claimed not to speak
Spanish, but it became clear after working with him with the help of a translator that he simply prefers not to. Don Cósimo's wife, Doña Amalia, has helped
out during our interviews. She is considerably younger than Don Cósimo and
helps him collect and prepare his medicines. She is almost always busy em-
broidering, and her work earns an important part of the family's income. The
hum of her foot-powered sewing machine accompanied interviews with Don
Cósimo. She defers to him and rarely offered any personal comments during
my visits to their house, although I feel that she is quite knowledgeable.

Don Tomás took my husband and me to meet Don Cósimo one afternoon.
At that time he was living in a house that appeared to date from the colonial
era. The house was showing its age, but the *solar* (house plot) was immaculate. The few parts of the yard that were not planted with something medicinal or ornamental were carefully raked. Don Tomás explained that Don
Cósimo cultivates the medicinal plants he uses most often, so that he will not
have to go looking for them in the woods each time he needs them. Don
Cósimo cures on a full-time basis. That afternoon a woman carrying a fever-
ish baby arrived after us and waited to see him.

It was a short first visit. Although I understood no Maya at the time, I could
tell that Don Tomás was asking Don Cósimo to work with me and was explaining
what I had in mind. Don Cósimo was preparing *balche* (ceremonial wine made
from the fermented bark of a leguminous tree, *Lonchocarpus longistylus* Pittier
[figure 26]), and he offered me some. I was thrilled to be tasting this ancient
Maya drink, used in agricultural rituals, and said so. I was also worried by the
fact that it was fermenting in an old tin washtub covered by a leaf-strewn
piece of screen. I barely tasted the *balche,* and then passed the rest of my
share to my husband, an action that I could see cost me points with Don
Cósimo. I had said to him that I felt honored to try this drink that I had heard
so much about, and then I gave my glass of it away after only a tiny sip.

Don Cósimo cures with plants and massage, conducts agricultural rituals,
and also tells fortunes with his *sastuns.* Conducting agricultural rituals and using
sastuns are what I have come to consider hallmarks of a *h-men* (literally "one
who does" or "one who makes"), but Don Cósimo says he is not a *h-men,* and
is "just a *yerbatero.*" This was contradicted by the comments of some residents of

a nearby town, who were working as laborers on an archaeological dig with an archaeologist acquaintance of mine. These people said that there were two *h-mens* who were basically in competition locally: Don Cósimo and a man who lives near the town of Chan Kom, fifteen kilometers southeast of Pisté. Don Cósimo's patients seem to come from the town of Pisté and the surrounding *ranchos*. Several of his neighbors refer to him as *"el doctor."*

Don Cósimo is the oldest curer I have worked with. Working with him was a completely different experience from the vigorous hiking through the woods to collect plants that I became accustomed to with both Don Tomás and Don Pedro. When he needed a plant that he did not have growing in his yard Don Cósimo sent either of his two sons off to find and gather it. Especially during our first sessions together, the boys would gather sterile sections of a plant or a handful of its leaves. They were not used to my demands for plants suitable for voucher specimens, and they clearly resented being sent back on return searches for intact flowering or fruiting specimens. Likewise, Don Cósimo was often reluctant to uproot an herb so that I could make a specimen of it. I struggled to explain that the ideal was to collect several specimens of each plant. Although I was paying for his time, I was also depleting Don Cósimo's living pharmacy! We struggled to accommodate each other, often wordlessly.

Like the other mostly monolingual Yucatec Maya curers, Don Cósimo's contact with foreigners has been limited. He had a bad experience with a gringo who came to learn about plant medicine from him several years before I met him. This person had reneged on payment for the lessons. When we began working together he was concerned that I would do the same thing. Because I had read and heard that a "true" curer was one who was disinterested in money, and both Don Tomás and Don Pedro always tried to refuse the small wages I could offer them, I felt affronted that Don Cósimo would insist on my paying him "up front" before each of our sessions together. This attitude seemed aggressive to me and at odds with the gentle and reserved person whom I glimpsed during those frustrating first meetings where I depended completely on a translator who found plant medicine antiquated. Don Cósimo listened intently to the questions I asked in Spanish and often surprised me by replying in Spanish before the translator could transform my question into Maya. Doña Amalia has taken on the role of language facilitator since those first sessions.

Even though we have known each other for five years now, it still surprises me that Don Cósimo has voluntarily shown me his *sastuns* several times, extracting them from a small velvet bag that hangs to one side of his home altar. He spoke frankly about his life and the manner in which he acquired his skills. Don Cósimo was eighteen and living in the pueblo of Chilub when he learned the work of curing. In Chilub he dreamed nightly for two years of a little old man who taught him where to look for his *sastuns,* how to conduct agricultural rituals, and all about medicine, including what have become his curing specialties.

During our tape-recorded interviews Don Cósimo listed his specialties. They included treating *canceres* (external tumors and sores), children who have been given the evil eye, fevers, *vientos malos* (evil winds), and infertility in women. At the end of the two-year period, the little old man of Don Cósimo's dreams informed him that now he was ready to cure, that he was ready to conduct his first *primicia* ("first fruit" ceremony).

Don Cósimo says that, although he was "ashamed" because many people were present for the ceremony, and he was unsure that all would go well, the work was not at all difficult, and he enjoyed doing it. After this first public ceremony, he was asked to perform the ceremony called *loh* (which protects a village from evil winds). He did so successfully, and afterward he always had work. He was never again "ashamed to do the work of curing." Treating broken bones and midwifery are the only types of curing that he does not do. Don Cósimo is the only curer I have met who tells fortunes, an activity that serves to augment his income. He passes certain of his *sastuns* over a candle's flame and then "reads" what he sees within.

Don Cósimo laughingly explained that at the time he began to cure and conduct ceremonies, he used to "be ashamed to be around women." He said that their presence worried him more "than doing the work." He described the behavior of some of the women who attended his early ceremonies as "shameless," although he did not elaborate on what this behavior was. He added that when he got over his shyness, he scolded them for their evil ways. Don Cósimo was a bachelor longer than most.

Don Cósimo has changed houses twice since I met him. With each move, he and his family have moved farther away from the town center. I interpreted this as an indication that they were moving down rather than up the social ladder, but others have pointed out that their newest house is their own and is not a rental property like the others, so that they interpret the latest move as a step up. The house itself is a small structure, with both roof and walls supplemented by odd pieces of tin and cardboard. It is used primarily for sleeping and cooking, with much of the family's daily activities taking place in the yard behind the house. There Don Cósimo tends to his patients, and his wife does her sewing under a shady tree. Doña Amalia's son has married and brought his wife and infant son to live with them. I do not think that he has helped make *milpa* or added to the family's resources. It seems to me that Don Cósimo looks frailer and has had fewer patients each time I have been to visit him, but I hope that I am wrong.

Don Aldo

If Don Cósimo lives the most precariously of the curers I have come to know, Doctor Aldo surely holds up the other end of the financial continuum, because he is owner of the town's pharmacy and has received Western medical training and titles through the Mexican government. Don Aldo, a native of Guerrero state, is the only non-Maya practitioner I have come to know. He is included here because his treatments include plants known and used by Maya practitioners, as well as European homeopathic remedies.

Several townspeople had spoken to me about Doctor Aldo before I had the chance to meet him. They pointed out the pharmacy on the main street in town and told me how to find Don Aldo's *consultorio* (dispensary), where a very large and intimidating German shepherd patrolled the fenced and gated yard. When I met Don Aldo, he was giving an English lesson to a small group of adults on the patio of his yard. I interrupted the lesson, was seated in the waiting room, and waited.

Don Aldo is in his early forties. His working uniform consists of jeans and an ironed shirt. He is one of the few people in Pisté who dress this way. He has a round unlined face and an energetic manner. He agreed to contribute to my survey just moments after I introduced myself to him. Our conversations have since taken place in his *consultorio,* an ordered space containing office furniture, an examining table, framed diplomas, and other trappings of "modern" medicine. Sailor, the German shepherd, wanders in and out at will, seeking the comfort of the fan-cooled air and the cement floor.

Interviews suggest that Don Aldo feels he is fulfilling a predetermined course in life. It was his fate, his destiny, to come to Yucatan, establish a practice, and become involved with traditional Maya medicine. Although he is scientific in his approach to testing specific uses of plants, a mystical bent surfaces in conversation again and again. For example, he stated that although dogs have intelligence and emotions, "plants have only emotions; they don't think, but they can communicate with you. We [human beings] have still more things: a spirit, an energy, as well as intelligence and emotions."

It was fascinating, and in some sense reassuring, to converse with another non-Maya person about traditional curing and curers during my time in Pisté. Our talks provided another perspective on the subject. Don Aldo said that,

> *h-mens* know how to establish something like a chemical connec-
> tion with the plants . . . you have to ask them, but I do not know how to
> ask them. The *h-men,* what he does is he asks the plant to cure you. . . . A
> plant is connected to the same flow of life as we are. All the plants of
> the earth are connected with the same flow of energy, with *la vida,*
> and we are the same. We aren't connected with the same direct

connection as the plants, but we are connected—isn't that so?

Don Aldo balances his mystical philosophy, or understanding of the world, with his scientific training and methods of testing plant medicines. He believes that the differences of opinions among allopathic practitioners, homeopaths, and those who utilize herbal medicines are mostly ego-related:

> It is a form of prejudice; the imagination doesn't grow. Nobody challenges a doctor. It's like the story of the emperor *desnudo* (the emperor with no clothes)—it's the same. How can we evolve like this? I know that there are many people who think like me, eminent doctors, that we have to transform, experiment. A doctor can't be only a writer of kitchen recipes. A prescription is like a kitchen recipe; we have to investigate, look further, experiment more.

Don Aldo reiterated that investigating nontraditional medicine requires tolerance and openness on the part of a Western practitioner:

> Many doctors have gone to study shamans, *yerbateros, h-mens.* I've seen it. Even if they cure, it doesn't touch them like that. They never say "this works—why?" Because we are talking again about prejudice— "I am a doctor; they are just people. It is a trick," they say. But it isn't, if there is something positive that I can learn from a person. Why not learn? To learn something, you have to reach a compromise; be it spiritual, shamanic, magic, or scientific. Are you going to cure with this? Is it going to help? Then don't lose it. If it works, don't let it go.

Don Francisco and Doña Francisca

If Don Aldo is the most loquacious of all the curers surveyed for this book, Don Francisco is perhaps the least. This could be due to the fact that I have only worked with him on two occasions, and on the second of these, he was thoroughly intoxicated on *balche* wine, having just returned from conducting a *kex* (change) ceremony. His wife, and working partner, Doña Francisca, seems to be quiet by nature. They live in a thatched house off the main road not far from Kaua and see patients in a separate structure next to their house. Don Francisco keeps regular hours on Tuesdays and Fridays, the days traditionally held to be most propitious for curing, and can be summoned at other times from his fields in case of emergencies and unannounced visitors such as Don Tomás and myself.

That first day, after Don Tomás directed us to the house of Don Francisco and Doña Francisca, we waited for two hours or so while a small child ran out to a distant field and summoned Don Francisco. He came all the way back, bathed quickly, and received us as though it had been no inconvenience at all. He is a robust man in his early fifties. Within minutes, he said that he was perfectly willing to teach me about plants and Maya medicine, and we made an appointment to return on the following Tuesday. Before we left, Don Francisco performed a *limpio* for each of us. This was a much more elaborate version than the one performed by Don Pedro. Don Tomás and I took turns being seated in front of Don Francisco's small altar laden with multiple crosses and images of Jesus and various saints, including one called St. Eustaquio, who Don Tomás explained was the "patron of the deer." I wonder whether this saint might be the Catholic equivalent of the *kuilob kaaxob* (guardians of the uncultivated forest), or perhaps the *zip* (a class of supernaturals who are the masters of the deer). The large, new poster of the Virgin of Guadalupe suspended over all the above was the recent gift of a group of curers from Mexico City who had come to study with Don Francisco.

Don Francisco used freshly cut branches of *sip che* (*Bunchosia swartziana* L.) and water that had been previously blessed in his efforts to sweep away any evil winds or spirits that had been afflicting us. His oration was primarily in Maya, but the protective powers of many Catholic saints were invoked along with the guardians of the four cardinal directions.

While he prayed, Don Francisco made the sign of the cross on top of the head of the patient, then on the nape of the neck, and finally in front of the patient's chest. Then he "sweeps" the patient (that is, continues making crosses with a handful of leaves that have been sprinkled with the holy water) in the same places. The "sweeping" continues all around and down the patient's body. Finally, Don Francisco dips his fingers into the holy water and traces still more crosses onto the same spots, as well as on the patient's palms and feet. Even though my feet were crossed, he swept my left foot first: the same order was maintained during Don Tomás' *limpio*. Don Francisco learned how to perform this ceremony and all the others in his repertoire though dreams.

Don Francisco stated explicitly that it was the *Balams* who "showed me how to cure." Although he referred to them in the plural, he said that he dreamed every night "of a little old man" who "taught him how to use crystals, more or less how to work." This personage instructed Don Francisco on how to perform the *kex, ch'a chaac, loh,* and other traditional ceremonies. He does not do massage, but dispenses plant medicine.

Doña Francisca arrived quietly sometime during the *limpios*. She appears to be about the same age as her husband. She is a midwife and "knows plants." She learned how to use them through a series of dreams in which a little old woman appeared nightly to instruct her. She and her husband invited me to return and "learn the manner in which they work." The pair work together collecting and drying plants for use in treatments. They both say I should improve my Maya so that I can make "a stronger connection" when I return. I was unsure whether they meant to them, or to the *Balams*. I was struck by the open and accepting reception Don Tomás and I received from this husband and wife team.

On the return visit, the same invitations were once again extended. Perhaps because Don Francisco was so intoxicated, Doña Francisca seemed to take a more active part in our conversation. Their eldest daughter, a woman in her thirties, joined the meeting. Like her mother, she is a midwife. I came equipped with a list of plant species previously collected in Yucatan, along with their primary usages, with the idea of interviewing the pair to determine whether they were familiar with the common names of the plants. It was mostly Doña Francisca whom I interviewed that day, but she and her husband conferred on many plant names I asked about. They were familiar with almost all the common names of the plants I had on my list and used most of them in the same way, or ways, as did Don Tomás, Don Pedro, and Don Cósimo. Husband and wife were visibly pleased when their uses were the same as those of the previously interviewed curers.

Don Francisco took a rather erratic part in this interview, reeling in and out of the house, sometimes returning with handfuls of plants we had discussed. At one point, he came in with a handful of something, which he playfully shook in my face. Doña Francisca reprimanded him and explained that the plant could cause a rash like that produced by *chechem (Metopium brownei)*. He invited Don Tomás and me to go with him to visit the curers from central Mexico.

On the way home, Don Tomás and I discussed the role of *balche* in traditional Maya ceremonies. His interpretation is that the consumption of this beverage, which is an emetic and is hallucinogenic if consumed in large enough quantities, serves to "open the mind of the curer" and make him more receptive to the communications/wishes of the *Balams* and other spirits or supernaturals. This conceptualization has also been recorded among the Lacandon Maya of Chiapas, Mexico. In *Life, Ritual, and Religion Among the Lacandon Maya*, author Jon McGee (1990:75) states that

> Drinking balché confers the ritual purity necessary to participate in ceremonies where the gods are present in a godhouse. At the same time, intoxication on balché induces the transcendental state that allows men to have personal interactions with their deities.

Doña Flor

I have only known Doña Flor for a short time, but from the first moments of our meeting her warm reception made me feel as though we had known each other for years. She is a beautiful woman who does not look her age, which must be about seventy-five years. She is the aunt of Doña Luz, who is in her early sixties. She is a widow who lives alone, supporting herself with her midwifery and other curing skills. She is the only independent woman curer that I have met, having learned the art of delivering babies as a girl from her mother and her mother's friend. From conversations, it seems as though Doña Flor's late husband was her partner, as is Doña Francisca to Don Francisco and Doña Amalia to Don Cósimo. However, the difference is that Doña Flor's career as a curer began before her marriage and continues now after it. If Doña Amalia, for all her knowledge, functions in a subservient role of helper to her husband, and Doña Francisca seems to be much more of an equal partner to her husband, I would say that Doña Flor represents the other end of the spectrum, although it is difficult to say if that was the case while her late husband was alive.

The way I met Doña Flor was a surprise to me. I had already become close with her niece, Doña Luz, who is married to Don Pedro and lives in Pisté. Over the course of several years I had asked repeatedly about the existence of midwives in and around Pisté. Doña Luz was among those who insisted that there were no such persons. Many of the women I got to know talked to me about the advantages of the government-run clinic in Valladolid over the old-fashioned midwives, especially in regard to delivering babies. One of these was Doña Luz' daughter, my friend Mariela.

One day during a visit when I was lucky enough to have secured a rental car, Don Tomás asked me if I could take Mariela to see her great-aunt who lived near Chan Kom. He explained that this lady was a midwife, and he hoped that she could help cure Mariela of a recurring infection that she had suffered for some time. I was delighted to provide transportation and finally meet a midwife. Redfield and Villa Rojas (1962:76) described the midwife as "the most important secular professional among women in Chan Kom," and therefore, by extension, to women in Yucatan. I had been looking forward to working with a female practitioner.

Mariela had been to the clinic in Valladolid several times for treatment but had found no relief. Perhaps her great-aunt's medicine was the last option left. Perhaps to Doña Luz, a church elder with little tolerance for "old superstitions," her aunt was a bit of an embarrassment, certainly a poor relation who lived out away from town. But no matter; we were going to go see her. Both Don Tomás and Mariela were sure that she would be happy to talk to me. They were right.

Very early one morning Don Tomás, Mariela, their little daughter Marina, and I headed for Doña Flor's house. It is a traditional Maya house, with a small area sectioned off from the main living area by a curtain that serves as Doña Flor's "office." Doña Flor speaks Spanish well, and she does so continuously and rapidly. She welcomed me as a friend of her great-niece and within moments had invited me to come back and study plant medicine with her as soon as possible. She warned me that we would have to spend days hiking around in the forest to find some of the rarer species and grinned broadly when I said that I liked walking in the woods.

Doña Flor has a very forthright attitude that is visible in all her actions: from the way she walks to the way she examines a patient. She is not brusque, but she is matter-of-fact. After learning of her great-niece's medical problem, she had Mariela strip to her petticoat and lie down on some burlap sacks after banishing Don Tomás from the house. She proceeded to palpate Mariela's belly in a way that seemed uncomfortable. Within minutes, she had a diagnosis: Mariela had an infected ovary that was causing the discomfort and discharge. She said that the ovary felt hard and larger than normal.

After explaining to both husband and wife what herb should be used in the treatments and how to prepare it, she turned her attention to me. She agreed to do an interview with me about her life and medicine. She explained that she had had to learn about "how to treat all the illnesses of poor people" in a way that was a deliberate reference to the difference in our status as she saw it. It became clear to me that in her dealings with Western-trained physicians Doña Flor had felt their attitude of superiority, but her faith in the efficacy of traditional medicine remains firm. Several times she stated that "natural medicine" is as good as, or superior to, Western-style medicines. At least twice during the interview, she seemed to feel she had said everything that needed to be said, asking me "What else do you want to know?" Finally, Doña Flor slipped completely into rapid Maya, the conversation turned to family news, and the interview ended. I had a hard time explaining that I could not specify a date when I would return to begin my lessons.

Before we left, I offered to photograph Doña Flor. This time, we were all banished from the house while she washed and changed for the occasion. She put on the bright blue hair-tie that I had given her. The photographs show her standing just outside the doorway of her house. She invited her neighbor to join her for two shots. Although I mailed the photos to Mariela as soon as I returned to the United States, they still have not been delivered over a year later. Doña Flor does not live in a place easily accessible by public transportation, but it is not far from Pisté. Mariela wrote to say that she had not been able to find the prescribed herbs and had not had the chance to deliver the photos. Her condition had neither improved nor worsened. I find myself puzzling over the relationship between the midwife and the rest of her family.

The Curers as a Group: Similarities and Differences

The curers discussed here are all herbalists to differing degrees. Plant medicine is the most obvious common thread that weaves through the lives of the curers I have come to know. It may be more or less important in terms of the individual's total curing repertoire, but it is always present.

With the exception of Don Aldo, with his biomedical training and later auto-didactic explorations of both Maya medicine and European homeopathy, all the curers I have worked with can be said to have learned their skills in one of two ways: either they learned voluntarily, from an older family member or close friend, or they learned through dreams. The next chapter discusses these two main methods of acquiring curing skills and examines the personal experiences of the curers as they learned their craft. Variations in curing specialties will be discussed in chapter 5.

What does an interest in plant medicine imply about the curers? All, with the exception of Don Aldo, grew up in rural areas where old traditions are strong. Certainly, they respect the traditions of their grandparents, but this is not to say that they are rigid conservatives. The curers whom I have come to know are remarkably flexible when it comes to incorporating new ideas, medicines, and techniques into their practices and lives. They value the old ways and accept what they think is worthwhile of the new. Conversely, Don Aldo values Western medicine and is also willing to explore traditional Maya medicine.

All the curers interviewed have stressed that they enjoy their work. They like to help people. As a group, they are good listeners, compassionate, open-minded, and possessed of good memories. When I asked each of them what they thought a person needed to become a curer, they answered unanimously that the most important thing was a desire to learn and apply oneself, coupled with a positive attitude.

Several of the curers said that it was good that I was learning about Maya curing so that I could practice in my country and help people there. Their willingness to work with me and share their cultural heritage initially came as a surprise. There was only one traditional practitioner who refused to have anything to do with me. She was a specialist whose entire busy practice is based upon her treatment of eye complaints. Taxis from Mérida and Cancún waited in the street in front of her house in the town of Dzitás. Don Tomás and I were ushered into a room with dark green walls and a row of chairs. She was cordial, and we seated ourselves to watch as she treated several patients. The treatment was always the same. She dipped pieces of cotton or cloth into a bottle and then squeezed a couple of drops into each of the patient's eyes. I think that it must have stung, as the patients' eyes teared up, and they tried not to pull back in their chairs. Everything changed when it was my turn for treatment, and Don Tomás tried to explain that I just wanted to talk about curing. Her face hardened instantly. We must be trying to make off with her secrets! Don Tomás and I had no choice but to beat a hasty retreat from her office. He said that she was "egotistical," the same word he used when describing another curer who practices on the coast near Tulum and is known for his protective and territorial attitude.

I would characterize the curers I have come to know in Yucatan as accepting and open. I have no way of knowing whether members of any other occupational group of Yucatec Mayas, say shoemakers or embroiderers, would have treated me the same way. Redfield and Villa Rojas (1962:75–76) suggest that curers are reclusive, uncanny people with a mystical bent who would be unlikely to share their knowledge with an outsider. My experience in Yucatan has been different.

I asked each curer if there are some types of illnesses that plant medicine cures more effectively than other kinds of treatment. Not surprisingly, evil eye and evil winds were frequently named. The curers who mentioned these diseases added that "doctors can't cure those at all." Snakebite, *pasmo* (literally, "chills"), and *bilis* (literally, "bile" or "biliousness") were mentioned along with fever, dysentery, and rheumatism. Don Aldo stated that plant medicine is superior for the treatment of chronic illnesses, because there are fewer secondary effects that accompany its use. Chapter 6 will examine the set of plants most frequently used or mentioned by the curers in this book.

CHAPTER FOUR
Acquiring Curing Skills

Apart from the unique case of Don Aldo, who went to medical school as part of a Mexican government training program and later learned about plant medicine through exposure to Maya practitioners and books on European homeopathic remedies, the remaining six practitioners surveyed acquired their curing skills in one of two different ways. Three of them learned about curing from a knowledgeable older relative or friend of the family during a lengthy, gradual, and rather informal process that took place over a period of years. The other three learned how to cure through strikingly similar dreams, in which an elderly person of the same sex as the potential healer appeared nightly for a variable period of time and provided instruction until the dream-teacher pronounced them "ready to cure."

Although the curers surveyed for this book obviously represent a small sample, I was surprised to find that none of them had learned by apprenticing themselves to renowned (but unrelated) practitioners. This method of skill acquisition through apprenticeship was the preconceived model that I brought with me to this research, due perhaps in equal parts to ideas internalized from historical models of medieval European society, the books of Carlos Castañeda, and the existing literature on the subject.

Redfield and Villa Rojas' (1962) work, *Chan Kom: A Maya Village*, is a classic ethnography of a Yucatec Maya village. I suspect that what the authors recorded about curing in Chan Kom over sixty years ago was probably representative of curing in Pisté or any of the other small towns of Yucatan at that time. As previously mentioned in chapter 2, this is an essential part of their thesis; Chan Kom represented an archetype of all other towns in the area that were equally distant (in both a cultural and a geographical sense) from Mérida, the "modern" capital of Yucatan, and the tribally organized settlements of Quintana Roo. Redfield and Villa Rojas (1962:75) noted a tendency for the *h-men* (which they translate variously as "shaman" and "priest"—the former term is more appropriate) to pass his vocation from father to son but also mentioned cases where "persons of seclusive or mystical temperament seek out famous shamans and become their apprentices." They describe a formal period of training lasting one year, during which the student learned about orations, plant medicine, and diagnosing illness. The apprenticeship was then completed by an initiation ceremony. The latter acquisition pattern sounds similar to the process Arvigo (1994) experienced more recently in Belize with the elderly Maya curer Eligio Pantí. I have not encountered anything similar. My data are closer to the pattern described by William F. Hanks. Although the focus of his work is linguistic, Hanks recorded the performances of a single shaman living near the town of Oxkutzcab and studied his practice between 1980 and 1981. Hanks (1996:174) reports that "Yucatec shamans do not undergo standardized training" and may learn their skills through apprenticeships of variable lengths or by way of "dreams in which the individual travels to sacred places and has instructive encounters." I here compare my findings to those presented in the above-named sources and to Redfield's (1941) work, *The Folk Culture of Yucatan,* because these are the main sources of information on Maya curing that are either relevant in geographical and cultural terms or deal with the role of the practitioner in a somewhat different, and much more recent, setting (in the case of Arvigo).

Excepting the case of Don Aldo, whose extensive biomedical training sets him apart from the other curers and who will be discussed at the end of this chapter, the remaining practitioners surveyed learned to cure through an apprenticeship to an older curer or to a supernatural entity that recruited them through dreams. A discussion of their individual experiences follows. Those who learned through dreams did not seek out any sort of "vision"; on the contrary, they were "chosen" to learn by supernatural beings. Those who learned from an elder mentioned necessity as a motivating force in their decision to learn how to cure. All practitioners stressed that they enjoyed learning their skills, regardless of how they did so. The following *historias* and quotes from individuals were drawn from tape-recorded interviews.

Learning from Elders

Don Pedro began learning how to use healing plants from his father when he was about twelve years old. He said that by that age, he was going about in the countryside with his father to make *milpa* and hunt. During the course of their daily work, his father taught him about "natural medicine." Don Pedro's father, in turn, had learned from an herbalist from his hometown, Oxkutzcab, in the southwestern part of the peninsula. He moved his family to the Chichén Itzá area in order to find work with the archaeological expeditions excavating in the ruins. Don Tomás, Don Pedro's son-in-law, told me that Don Pedro's father was quite famous, but (curiously or modestly, I cannot say) Don Pedro denies this. Interestingly, Don Pedro says that his father learned about plant medicine from a man who had a book on the subject, which contained a history of medicinal herbs.

In response to my questioning, Don Pedro stated that this book was not one of the famous Chilam Balam books (a group of colonial manuscripts named for the towns in which they were found, containing differential amounts of divinatory, medicinal, and historical information) but was titled *Xiu, nada más.* (Xiu, nothing more). The Xiu family of southwestern Yucatan was a powerful force throughout the colonial epoch; indeed many legends deal with the bitter rivalry between the Xiu lineage and that of the Cocoms of Chichén Itzá. The word *xiu* also means "herb" or "plant" in Yucatec Maya, so the title of this intriguing book may refer to the subject matter rather than the Xiu lineage.

When Don Pedro's family moved, "We began to know the herbs that he had shown [him?], all the classes of herbs that I have shown you ... a little bit [laughs]." Don Pedro noted that the plants of each region of Yucatan are different. According to him, the plants of the state of Yucatan are most different from those of the state of Quintana Roo. The latter receives much more rain than Yucatan, and even though the same species may grow in both places, those of Quintana Roo often grow so large as to be almost unrecognizable.

Don Pedro's repertoire of healing methods also includes *sobadas* (massage), but this was a self-taught skill. *"No más que yo aprendí"* (I just learned it.) He says that he began to do massage on himself when his hand or bones were hurting from working in his fields or in the ruins of Chichén Itzá where, like his father, he found employment. The men who came to work at Chichén Itzá often stayed on, moving their families to Pisté.

Don Tomás comes from a family of curers. I have already noted that he describes his uncle, his grandfather, and his great-grandfather as *h-mens*. Don Tomás emphasized that he, like his mother and father before him, learned how to work with plants out of necessity. Xtojil was (and is) a fairly isolated place; as he put it, "We learned about medicinal plants from my parents as there was no one to cure us there." His mother gave birth to twelve children at the *rancho,* aided only by her husband; "as there was no midwife or anyone nearby ... we had to learn of necessity, we had to learn to help others."

Like Don Pedro, Don Tomás learned about the plants that cure by accompanying older male relatives out to work in the fields and while hunting in the woods. He said, "As I went about with my father, and I liked the plants a lot, I studied the form in which they worked ... learning which class of plant was good for curing ... what plant they used if some accident happened, what kind of plant to use in emergencies, to serve us." He does not do massage. Don Tomás has also learned quite a lot about women's medicine and has assisted at births in his family. He considers women's medicine to be one of the most effective components of the traditional Maya medical system.

Doña Flor is the third curer surveyed who learned from an elder. She learned about midwifery and plant medicine primarily from her mother, whom she half-jokingly describes as a *x-men* (the *"x"* prefix often denotes "female" in Yucatec Maya). Her mother was a midwife in her hometown, Dzeal. Doña Flor said that she began to help her mother with her work delivering babies when she was "still a girl." She also credits her mother's *comadre* (godmother or close friend) with teaching her midwifery, in particular, how to deal with babies who are in a breech position. Doña Flor has delivered ninety-one babies and remembers them all.

Doña Flor learned more about plant medicine from her late husband, who specialized in treating snakebite. She also attended classes on midwifery given by Instituto Nacional Indigenista (INI) in the city of Valladolid and has "worked with" a well-known local doctor (who has Hispanicized his name from the Maya surname Ek [star] to become Dr. Estrella) who practices in the town of Kaua. Apparently, this doctor used to make "house calls" to isolated *ranchos,* but now remains at Kaua and has arranged a sort of referral system whereby Doña Flor informs him of potentially difficult cases. I am not certain if she brings those cases to him or if he comes to her house-cum-office. As noted previously, Doña Flor, unlike Don Pedro and Don Tomás, sees patients from outside the family on a regular basis in her home.

Doña Flor is very proud of her association with Dr. Estrella and the INI clinic, but her pride is tempered with skepticism. For example, she has either witnessed or assisted with Caesarean operations but maintains that the position of a breech baby can be changed with the use of plants and massage in order to avoid the procedure. "Sometimes the baby is twisted in the womb. And if you don't turn it, they will cut you, the doctors. It's not necessary if you know the medicine of the plants. It's good."

Learning through Dreams

I have already mentioned that three of the practitioners surveyed learned their curing skills through dreams. Their experiences were quite similar. The two male practitioners who learned curing this way either describe themselves or are described by others as *h-mens.* As such, they conduct agricultural ceremonies dealing with the Maya gods and diagnose and treat illnesses using both empirical and magical-religious means. They employ the use of special paraphernalia such as *sastuns* in their work. Thus their work encompasses the roles we North Americans would perhaps divide into separate categories of practitioners: doctor, priest, therapist, and witch. The roles and functions of the *h-men* are discussed in detail in the next chapter.

Redfield and Villa Rojas (1962:75) characterize the *h-men* as the most important of the sacred professionals found in the village hierarchy of Chan Kom, and they note that although "the priestly functions" of the *h-men* are the exclusive domain of males, the wife of a *h-men* is often an herbalist, as is Doña Francisca, the third practitioner who learned her calling though dreams. She is both an herbalist and a midwife.

These three practitioners all experienced a series of dreams, night after night, for a period of one to three years, in which a little, old person appeared (an elderly man appeared to the men, and an elderly woman appeared to the woman) to instruct the dreamers on how to cure, which plants to use, and in the cases of the men, how to find and use *sastuns*. The many uses of crystals are discussed in detail in the next chapter.

Doña Francisca says that "a little grandmother" began appearing to her in her dreams when she was a young woman and "taught her how to be a midwife, how to do massage." The term *sobadora* (a female massage practitioner) is often synonymous with the word *partera* (midwife), as massage is seen as an intrinsic part of a midwife's work. Doña Francisca's dreams lasted for about two years. Her experiences represent a departure from what Redfield and Villa Rojas (1962:72–73) describe in Chan Kom, where they suggest that midwifery is a skill passed on to "assistant-disciples" during a fairly lengthy period of training.

When I asked Doña Francisca's husband, Don Francisco, how long his dreams lasted, he responded with "until I learned it all." "All" in his case meant learning about plant medicine, how to conduct the rainmaking ceremony and other Maya rituals, and how to find and use crystals. He described the man he saw nightly in his dreams as being very old, with white hair and a beard. He stressed that he enjoyed the dreams and learning the work, saying "I enjoyed it, all of it." Don Francisco does not do massage or deliver babies; this is the work of his wife and curing partner, Doña Francisca. I have not met a male curer who makes delivering babies and administering prenatal care part of his curing repertoire, although Don Cósimo, the last of the curers surveyed who learned their work through dreams, treats infertility in women, and Don Tomás has described quite a bit about birth-related medicine (how to assuage labor pains, how to treat the umbilical cord after it is cut, and so forth), knowledge he picked up from his mother and other female relatives.

Since I have known Don Cósimo longer than Don Francisco and Doña Francisca, it is not surprising that he discussed his dream education in more detail than they did. He began to dream when he was eighteen years old. His dreams also lasted for two years. Every night a little old man with very white hair and a beard, wearing the *delantal* (apron) of "the old ones" appeared to him and showed him "all the herbs to cure all types of infirmities" and where to look to find his personal crystals. When I asked if the man he saw was "like a person" (meaning in his appearance), he replied that he saw him "with his mind, in his dreams."

After two years of dreams, the little old man told Don Cósimo he was ready to do his first ceremony, a *primicia*, where thanks are given to all the appropriate supernaturals for a bountiful harvest. Despite his apprehensions, all went well, and soon after Don Cósimo officiated at a *loh* ceremony (which protects a village from evil winds). After that, he always "had work." Don Cósimo's work includes massage "when the people ask for it or need it," but he does not deliver babies. Don Cósimo's curing specialties include treatments for *ojo* (evil eye), fevers, *vientos* (evil winds), external cancers, and infertility. Since crystals are often used for diagnosis, I asked him if he used his *sastuns* to determine whether the man or the woman is "at fault" in the last named infirmity; Don Cósimo surprised me by saying, "For that, one goes to the doctor"!

The Balams: A Supernatural Connection

The descriptions of the beings who appeared to show the two male dreamers, Don Cósimo and Don Francisco, how to cure resemble Redfield and Villa Rojas' (1962:113) description of the class of Maya deities known as *balams*. They are the guardians of both village and cornfield and are the recipients of many of the *h-men*'s offerings and prayers. They are characterized as "small old men, with white hair, wearing sandals, sombrero, and the rest of the local costume." The "local costume" at that point in time featured a sort of apron that men wore over their trousers. Hanks (1996:174) mentions that the shaman he interviewed was instructed by "guardian spirits" called "Jaguar Lords." One possible meaning of the word *balam* is "jaguar."

Although these beings or spirits are generally good to man, protecting his village from sickness and evil winds and his fields from theft or roaming animals, they have a dark side as well. As Redfield and Villa Rojas (1962:112–15) say:

> The *Balams* are also much to be feared. They are the uncanny beings of the night. When they cry out in the darkness, it is a sign that some one is going to die. They watch over lost children, but they return only a changeling . . . the idiot and the feebleminded are the children of the *Balam*. The *Balams* guard the *milpa*, but only if the owner gives to them the corn that is theirs and offers them the prayers they expect.

The *balams* are linked to curing in many of the stories one hears told in Yucatan. All the curers I have worked with have further elaborated on the connection between the *h-men* and the *balams*. They unanimously state that the *sastuns* are "the gift" of the *balams*, and provide the means of communicating with them and tapping into their powers. This stands in direct contrast not only to Redfield and Villa Rojas' (1962:76) statement that the crystals are the gift of the master curer to his student at the end of his training period but also to Arvigo's (1994) experience in Belize.

There are, however, similarities: In all three scenarios the initiate receives his or her *sastuns* from the teacher, whether the latter is a human being or a supernatural being. Some part of the teacher's skill seems to be thus conveyed to the student, and the crystals themselves symbolize this linkage and serve to validate the status of the initiate as a curer in his or her own right. The difference between receiving one's personal crystals from a supernatural entity rather than a human being could be likened to the difference between receiving a medical degree from Harvard Medical School versus a small state university. Differential degrees of status are accorded to the recipients.

Supernatural validation may be increasingly important in a rapidly changing society, especially if clinics and biomedical practitioners are increasingly sought out, and their brand of medicine replaces some of the more empirically oriented components of traditional Maya medicine. The aid of the owner of crystals may be sought only in those cases where problems or illnesses are considered supernatural or magical in nature.

Even in the early 1930s, Redfield and Villa Rojas (1962:112–13) noted that there seemed to be quite a bit of confusion in the minds of both laymen and professionals about the different classes of supernaturals who surround the Maya people of Yucatan. In particular, they noted a confusion (or blending) of the roles of the *balams* with those of the *chacs* (the rain deities) and the *kuilob kaaxob* (guardians of the forest and wild animals). Sixty years later, my own questions about the *balams* and their powers have revealed contradictory information and explanations. Regardless of this confusion of identities, it is clear that curers gain legitimacy and power through a supernatural connection.

Interestingly, Doña Francisca, the one woman who learned to cure from dreams, saw an elderly woman, rather than a man, who taught her the craft. Apart from the gender of the dream-teacher, her experiences were similar to those of Don Cósimo and Don Francisco; however, no one ever suggested that a *balam* could be female.

The *balams* show the dreamer where in the woods or fields he or she must go to look for their crystals. The *sastuns* signify that the owner has been approved of or selected in some sense by these beings. Places away from town, especially uncultivated forest, are the domain of the *balams*. They guide people to discover crystals in their environment. Don Cósimo found one of his crystals embedded in the fork of a tree. Others have found *sastuns* lying in their path on the ground.

Given the generally secretive attitude toward crystals, I was surprised when Don Cósimo volunteered to show me his collection. Some of his fifteen crystals were natural stones: one was blue and transparent, another dark and opaque "like onyx" as he described it. Two large glassy ones with carved facets had "the form of a rat and the form of a heart." The rat and the heart looked as though they could have been purchased in a department store, but when I asked him where he got them, he replied, "Where they told me to look, that's where I found them, on my way, in the *milpa*."

I myself have found bits of what appeared to be worked, faceted stone, perhaps obsidian, or some type of dark greenish-black quartz, out in the *milpas* of Don Tomás and Don Pedro. I hypothesize that there is an archaeological reason for their existence, because the stones appeared in an area that, even to my untrained eye, resembles a large structural platform of some kind. Don Tomás and Don Pedro both describe these blackish objects as "the arrows of the *balams*." To them, they are evidence that the *balams* have been driving away marauding animals. Again, this is quite similar to what Redfield and Villa Rojas (1962:113) recorded in Chan Kom. In the authors' description of the good things *balams* can do for men, they mention that "by night you may hear a high whistling sound; this is made by the *balams*, who are driving away evil winds or animals by shooting at them with fragments of obsidian or flint." These stones are called *tok* in Yucatec, which means "flint." They are said to have protective power. I believe that both obsidian and flint are nonlocal.

Don Aldo: An Eclectic Healer

The way in which Don Aldo acquired his curing skills is the most divergent from the patterns discussed above. The extensive Western medical training he received in the Mexican Navy sets him apart from the other curers surveyed, as does his use of homeopathic remedies of European origin. He employs some of the same traditional Maya herbal cures as do the other practitioners, but his scientific approach to these "alternative" treatments differs. He has been using a relatively small number of local plants in his treatments for several years now and believes that there is a place in modern medicine for them, "although not to the exclusion of everything else."

Don Aldo is certainly the wealthiest of the curers I have come to know in the Pisté area, but this is not to say that he is as wealthy as other government-trained medical doctors in Mexico. He owns the best-supplied pharmacy in the town of Pisté, and its earnings help to support his *consultorio*, which he operates on the basis of donations. He is a native of Guerrero state but does not use any traditional medicine from that part of the Republic. As he put it, "Prior to moving to Pisté, my reality was that of allopathic medicine; my thoughts always went in that direction." Don Aldo perceives his arrival in Yucatan and subsequent involvement in studying natural medicine in a somewhat mystical light, one that might be characterized as "New Age." As he put it:

> I was in Acapulco, working on a ship, when I heard the words "Quintana Roo." The words got my attention, the sound of them. There I was in the middle of the Republic; I didn't know Maya, *ni nada, ni nada*... simply that I wanted to go there.

According to Don Aldo, he was thinking about the intriguing-sounding

Quintana Roo at the moment when a memorandum arrived on the ship sending him to Chetumal in that very state. He says that at that time he had "no consciousness of plants, herbs, any of that. I was just concerned with my job, and that was that. I was in the military . . . I was transformed by the environment (of Yucatan) and all the rest of it."

From Chetumal, Don Aldo was sent to Tampico. Then he returned to Cancún, by way of the navy base in Isla Mujeres. After his time in the military, he was working in the Hotel Zone of Cancún when he went to visit the archaeological treasures of Chichén Itzá, which impressed him greatly. An acquaintance offered him the opportunity to invest in a small pharmacy in Pisté. He did so, without planning to move to the town.

> But something happened to me, my life began to change with all those trips to Pisté. People, employees, all said that I should stay there and help them. I noticed that life was different (here) than in the city. I went around the region, and some odd things happened, little things that changed the state of my *ánimo* (soul) . . . *¿no?* . . . I had two lives; one here, one there. The one here [Pisté] was more tranquil. I had to leave the one for the other . . . people here had no money, and I learned more compassion. There it was like a mechanical life, looking for money, all that.

Other transformations ensued. A visiting chiropractor from the United States was doing volunteer work in Cancún, and government officials asked Don Aldo if he might be able to help out with his good command of the English language and facilitate the work of the visiting doctor. It turned out that Don Aldo was impressed by the American's techniques, which included acupressure and other nontraditional components. This, Don Aldo claims, opened his eyes to the possibilities of non-Western medicine. Studying European homeopathic tomes provided more food for thought. He began giving rose infusions to treat depression, and to his surprise, they seemed to help the patients.

Then Don Aldo and his wife started a free clinic in the nearby community of San Felipe, "where there was a lack of facilities, a dearth of necessities." At the clinic, they relied on donated medicines from doctor friends. But then the economy took a turn for the worse, and they ran out of supplies. The couple decided to turn to plant medicine, "to use what we had." This theme of necessity echoes many of the statements by other curers who never had the option of access to Western medicine.

Don Aldo began keeping a notebook about local plants and their uses, focusing on the most accessible and cultivable species. The people of the community did not want to support Don Aldo's plan to construct a garden of medicinal plants; in fact, they wanted the pills and tablets that he could no longer supply.

Don Aldo and his wife closed the clinic in San Felipe and opened the *consultorio* in Pisté. He spent three months studying with a *h-men*. He continues to experiment with and test plant remedies. He often prescribes a plant remedy in conjunction with Western medicine. His opinion is that the two types of medicine work synergistically, performing much better together than either one alone. This compromise solution is indubitably more attractive to patients who prefer the higher-status "pills" to plant medicine.

Although I do not agree with all of Don Aldo's personal philosophy, I think that the work he is doing in documenting the use and results of herbal treatments is invaluable. He is doing what he can to improve the health of his adopted community, with a limited number of resources. He is an unusually open-minded and humane doctor.

I am fascinated by the way that Don Aldo and all the other curers I have come to know continue to incorporate new elements into their treatments. This trait of experimentation, or willingness to combine old and new therapies, exists regardless of the means by which the curers acquired their skills. Whether the practitioner learned from a family member or a medical school, or through dreams, it seems that curing in Yucatan is continuing to evolve, even as it retains elements that have been included in curing repertoires since the colonial epoch.

CHAPTER FIVE

Exploring the Spectrum of Curing Specialties: Common Practices

During the course of both field and library research on the curers of Yucatan, I became aware of a number of different terms that seemed to represent different kinds of curers or curing specialties. The first part of this chapter contains the results of research I conducted in order to understand the differences among them and determine whether the categories mentioned in the literature still exist. The following section examines common curing practices or components of individual practices. When I first began to work with Don Tomás, he mentioned three terms repeatedly: *h-men, dzadzac,* and *pulyah.* I began my investigation with them, first consulting *Chan Kom: A Maya Village* (Redfield and Villa Rojas 1962) and then eliciting definitions of these terms from curers.

Redfield and Villa Rojas (1962:71–77) claim that the *h-mens* were the shaman-priests of the village and that they were exclusively male. They served as intermediaries between men and supernaturals but were also usually herbalists. The *dzadzac* were male or female *(x-dzadzac)* herbalists. Often the *h-men*'s wife was an herbalist. Although women could not be *h-mens,* they might be either witches or *parteras.* The Spanish term *partera* was widely used at that time, with the Maya *x-hiikab* ("she who does massage") or *x-ilah-kohan* ("she who observes the sick") recorded as alternates. Midwives were exclusively female, and *kaxbaac* (bonesetters) were exclusively male. Males could be witches or *pulyahs* (sorcerers).

Essentially, the authors describe a hierarchical arrangement, with the categories "male" and "sacred" ranked above "female" and "secular." Clearly, the categories overlapped. My research was motivated by a typically Western impulse to sort out the categories in order to understand them better. I also hoped to learn something about how the curers saw themselves in relation to these categories.

The practice of midwifery and plant medicine overlap. A midwife is almost certainly also a *x-dzadzac* or *yerbatera* (herbalist). The two midwives I have come to know both use plant medicine and massage therapy as part of their prenatal and postpartum care; as I have already mentioned, the term *sobadora* literally means "masseuse."

Three of the male curers also utilized massage in their treatments. The male masseurs seem to focus on realigning bones and muscles in patients of both sexes. Don Cósimo states that he does some things "to stretch the bones" but that he does not deal with setting them at all, adding that "there are specialists for that." Male curers who do massage may be the direct descendants of Redfield and Villa Rojas' *kaxbaac*, although when Don Tomás described the practice of his father, he used another term, *utzkil a bac* (fixes your bone) rather than *kaxbaac*. Don Pedro and Don Cósimo also used the former term. I have not met any male practitioner whose entire practice consists of massage. Although Don Tomás and his father helped the women in their family give birth, I have not met a male midwife per se. Male curers rarely oversee pregnancies or attend births.

When I asked the three curers with whom I have worked the most, Don Tomás, Don Pedro, and Don Cósimo, to explain the difference in the meaning of the terms *dzadzac, h-men,* and *pulyah,* their responses provided an interesting point of comparison to what Redfield and Villa Rojas (1962:75) had recorded in Chan Kom.

The three curers agreed upon the following definitions: a *yerbatero/a* or *(x)dzadzac* (the Maya word was known to all but used infrequently) is simply a person, male or female, who knows about traditional plant medicine and uses it to cure people, often for a fee. So, also, is a *h-men*. The defining difference between a *yerbatero* and a *h-men* is that only the latter "works with" *sastuns* given him by the *balams*.

The first year that I worked with Don Tomás, I took notes as he described the relation between the *balams* and *sastuns*. His explanation went like this:

> *Balams* are the *Dueños del monte* (Masters of the Forest). They live in caves, and they bring winds. The crystals are a gift from them that you use for talking to them. *Balams* give power to men in the woods when they are fourteen or fifteen years old. Women can learn to use *sastuns* from a man in the family, but they do not receive power from the jungle. . . . *Balams* take care of you in the woods. When you hear whistles, they are caring for you, warning away animals. But you have to keep your mouth closed or the *balam*'s winds can enter. They do not like it if you answer their whistles; it is disobedient, as when a sergeant gives you an order and you disobey. *Sastuns* are used to communicate with the *balams*. Past, present, future, divining sicknesses—everything! They can tell you who gives you a bad sickness and give one back to them.

The crystals are the medium by which the *balams* may reveal information such as the cure for a specific illness or its source. They also prevent sickness or evil sent by another person from "sticking" to their owners. The crystals are a *defensa* (magical defense, guard), absorbing evil that might otherwise affect the curer. The *h-men* is a person who has established a connection to supernatural beings and whose work is sanctioned by them.

In addition to diagnosis and curing, the (male) *h-men* utilizes his crystals in conjunction with agricultural ceremonies, which take place in the fields or the uncultivated forest. In those settings, the crystals are used to locate game animals (who are protected by the *balams*) and underground water for use in agricultural ceremonies and to determine whether ritual foods baked in *pibs* (underground ovens) are completely cooked. Redfield and Villa Rojas (1962:170) recorded similar uses for crystals in Chan Kom. Several curers and townspeople have also told me that the *h-men* may also use his crystals to help locate lost children. Redfield and Villa Rojas (1962:114, 176) note that the *balams* care for strayed children but may return changelings in their places.

Don Tomás' perspective differed from that of Don Pedro and Don Cósimo on the definition of the term *pulyah*. The two last-mentioned curers maintained that a *pulyah* is a black magician, whereas Don Tomás stated that this is not necessarily true; he is simply "the most powerful with crystals." Don Tomás' interpretation also differs from that of Redfield and Villa Rojas (1962:74), who say that the role of *pulyah* is "incompatible" with that of the *h-men* and that they are "unacceptable" to the *balams* and other *yuntziloob* (agricultural deities). Don Tomás described the *pulyah* as:

> a specialist who never has relations with women or marries. He lives a solitary life apart from towns and refrains from eating salt, or taking part in dancing or other entertainments. They have the most powers, including the ability to cure diseases with just an application of their saliva. A woman cannot become a *pulyah*—that is condemned.

In his account, the *pulyah* is credited with exceptional curing abilities. It is unclear to me in what way a witch differs from a sorcerer. Redfield and Villa Rojas (1962:179) mention that salt is dangerous to witches, perhaps an example of the blending of two roles that were more distinct in the past. The use of salt to destroy witches or similar evil creatures is mentioned in Tzotzil folklore (e.g., Laughlin 1977:275–78), so it may be an old Maya belief. Steggerda (1941:69) notes that holy water and a handful of salt were placed inside the coffin of a man from Pisté whose funeral he attended in 1938. The significance of this action is not discussed, but perhaps it is related to protecting the deceased from some supernatural threat.

All the curers and many laypeople told me stories about *uayoob*. These people can turn themselves into a variety of animals, usually black ones, and go about doing *maldades* (evil things). They might spy on people, steal from them, or make love to them in their sleep. If they are killed in their animal forms, they turn back into people at the moment of death. One curer told me how he awakened to find a female witch in the form of a *tigrillo* (ocelot?) on his chest. He struggled to pull her off, but she was slippery! The witch left stains on his shirt. Another curer told me he had seen a male witch in the form of a black dog suspended in the air, eating food out of a storage basket that hung from his ceiling by a vine. Other witches are said to feed on human blood, like our vampires.

Witches can cause a variety of things to happen to people with whom they want to have fun or punish. Stories about witches provide much after-dinner entertainment. I was told that the town of Kan Xoc, near Valladolid, was known for its witches. If you do not behave well while you are visiting there, witches can cause chairs to "stick" to your buttocks when you arise from them, just as a joke. In Yaxuna, a witch went to ask the hand in marriage of a local girl. She and her parents were witches too. They rejected him as a suitor, and he began to feel bad after he went home. He felt a pain around his belly button, and wasps flew out! He in turn put a spell on her, and milk began to flow from her breasts, even though she was neither married nor pregnant. Witches also have the ability to wave their hands and transform people into snakes or make necklaces move from one person's neck to that of another.

These stories are amusing and scary in perhaps the same way as a ghost story is in this country, but the distrust of curers is a more serious matter. A curer may have a "dark side" and do many of the same things that people say "witches" do, such as transform themselves into animals, and cast (and reverse) evil spells. Steggerda (1943:25) mentions that accusations of witchcraft forced two *yerbateros* to move away from Pisté in 1933. Villa Rojas (1945:136) describes how in 1936 a woman curer was hanged in Quintana Roo after she was blamed for an epidemic of intestinal infection. The source of infection was later traced to contamination of the village's drinking water supply. The government may also persecute curers, although for different reasons. Don Tomás told me about a well-known curer from Quintana Roo who was jailed because the department of health thought that he was dispensing medicine without a license. This curer utilizes both a *sastun* and eggs for divining, and plant medicine for treatments.

Curing and witchcraft may be seen as two sides, light and dark, of the same coin. This duality often creates suspicion in the eyes of the curer's neighbors and townsmen and is the source of a major problem I have had in getting the curers to describe themselves. Eliciting abstract definitions of types of curers was an easy job. When it came to answering personal questions about how the curers saw themselves in terms of those definitions, there was a general tendency for them to deny specialized roles; all deprecated their own and usually contradicted both my own perceptions and those of local people who knew them. Are you what you call yourself? Or what your neighbors call you? This Rashomon-like phenomenon indicates that the sharply defined roles suggested by distinct names for different practitioners do not exist in reality. The roles are both fluid and overlapping.

Gender

As a woman, I have been particularly interested in learning if any of the areas of curing in Yucatan are gender specific. There seem to be only a few areas that are restricted by gender. Female midwives use a different kind of massage than do male masseurs. I have not met any women curers who do chiropractic massage, which appears to be an exclusively male domain. As previously mentioned, I have not met any male midwives practicing near Pisté, although I have heard that male midwives exist in the state of Campeche (personal communication, Don Edilberto Ucan Ek, former instructor of traditional plant use workshops in Zoh Laguna, Campeche State).[2]

Women may be herbalists or midwives, but they cannot be *pulyah*, although they may be witches. Whether or not a woman may be a *h-men* remains unclear. Interviews with several curers on this question yielded contradictory responses. Don Pedro said no. Don Cósimo said that women could use crystals and mentioned the name of a woman in a nearby town who uses them to "see the future." Don Tomás clarified his earlier statements and explained that women may establish a connection to the *balams* with a personal crystal, as had several of his female relatives, but they are prohibited from using them in the agricultural ceremonies. It is unclear to me whether a man must serve as the intermediary who receives the crystals and then shares them with a woman curer. Other interviews suggest that the crystals are very personal power objects.

Doña Flor described her mother as a *x-men,* but in a joking way. Several curers also jokingly(?) stated to others that I was studying to become one. Don Francisco and Doña Francisca seemed to think it possible for a gringa to do so, if she spoke Maya well enough. Don Tomás said that "the *balams* decide who will receive their gifts."

Neither of the two women curers in this book uses a crystal in her practice.

---

2. Campeche is experiencing a large influx of new residents coming from other Mexican states (especially Vera Cruz and Chiapas) and Guatemala. The male midwives may well be newcomers from outside Yucatecan traditions.

However, in *Sastun*, Arvigo (1994:113) describes how she received her *sastun* in Belize. Its receipt signaled to her teacher, Don Eligio Pantí, that she was now fully capable of handling spiritual problems and illnesses. This work seems to include divining sources of illness, exorcising evil spirits, and black magic (as in Yucatan), as well as enchanting personal objects and protective amulets. Arvigo's teacher explains that the *sastun* is a connection to nine (unnamed) celestial beings called "The Maya Spirits." Interestingly, Arvigo undergoes an initiation ceremony after the receipt of her crystal that is reminiscent of the one described in Chan Kom by Redfield and Villa Rojas (1962:76–77) for male initiates. It is unclear whether a female initiate is prohibited from any aspects of curing in Belize.

My dissertation director, Dr. Victoria Bricker (personal communication), has pointed out that since there is a feminine form of the term *h-men (x-men)* in Yucatec Maya, such roles may well exist for women in other communities. My limited data and Arvigo's account from Belize suggest the possibility that women may be participating in more aspects of curing today than in the past. The agricultural ceremonies may be the only part of the *h-men*'s role that remains taboo to women. Traditionally, women have been seen as agents of contamination and so are still prohibited from attending agricultural ceremonies, although they may prepare food offerings for them. Arvigo's teacher was not able to find an apprentice until she came along. Perhaps women are moving into new territory by default? If so, Redfield and Villa Rojas would certainly attribute the move to the ongoing process of secularization of Maya culture.

Hierarchy

Redfield and Villa Rojas' hierarchical arrangement of curers was helpful to me when I began this research. It gave me the linguistic clues I needed to begin to understand the spectrum of curing specialists in Yucatan. Other hierarchies of curers have been proposed since the time of Redfield and Villa Rojas, including those of Press (1977:454–64) and Romano (1965). Both of those authors have suggested a model in which knowledgeable neighbors who cure on a part-time basis represent the low end of the hierarchy, with regionally known full-time specialists, who may end up being venerated as folk saints, on the high end of it.

Arvigo (1994:123–24) describes a somewhat different hierarchy among the traditional healers of Central America:

> There are bonesetters, massage therapists, and snake doctors, who specialize in specific physical ailments. The next level consists of midwives, herbalists, and granny healers . . . , who are able to treat a variety of physical conditions. But there are few of the doctor-priests,

or H'mens, such as Pantí, who in the Maya tradition are able to treat the mind, body, and soul, regardless if the ailment began in the belly or the disquieted soul.

Arvigo's hierarchy reminds me of the one proposed by Redfield and Villa Rojas (1962:75–77), with the difference that women seem not to be prohibited from participating in the upper level of the hierarchy. Are these arrangements merely inventions of a person outside the culture attempting to understand the relationships of the roles, or do cultural insiders also perceive the relationships in that way? Although the curers were quite willing to discuss definitions of Maya terms referring to different types of practitioners, their responses did not suggest that they perceived them to be ranked categories in any way. The only direct reference to any specifically hierarchical arrangement has come from Don Tomás when he said that "the *h-men* works with crystals," and "the *pulyah* has more of those same powers." As objectionable as the fact may be to feminist scholars, Maya society is hierarchical in terms of male-female relationships. Perhaps I was expected to understand that women's curing is implicitly less valued than men's curing? The Maya curers with whom I worked have helped me to understand an idealized model of the kinds of curers in Yucatan. Like all models, the one they presented to me tends to have fewer ambiguities than the real-life situation suggests.

Common Curing Practices

Prayer

Prayer in a variety of forms is an important component of the practices of the curers in this book. Whom one prays to and how and when one does so differs from person to person. The following excerpts from interviews with the curers on their methods of prayer illustrate its many uses in curing. This was one of the most personal aspects of each person's practice, and some were unwilling to share their prayers with me. As Don Tomás said, "Every person who cures with plants has their own *milagros* (miracles); their own belief in which saints will help cure the sickness that a person has, to discover which plant to give them." Divulging personal prayers may detract from their efficacy. Don Cósimo told me that each person develops their own and that these are "for them alone." Interestingly, Don Tomás draws a distinction between the private prayers of the "person who cures with plants" and the public prayers of "those who work with the *balams*."

Don Pedro believes that faith is important to both curer and patient; both need to believe that the cure will work. In addition, "the person who is going to cure has to have a lot of faith in the plants as well; they have to think that they will cure the other person with these particular plants. One has to work with God because it is He who sowed all the seeds, yes!"

Don Pedro stated that one asks for God's help when searching for medicine, but not out loud:

> In one's mind, as you go to look for plants, if the first medicine does not
> provide a cure one looks for another class of plant. Sometimes one goes
> out into the countryside looking for a plant, and one goes around in
> circles without finding it. But when one is not looking for it, immediately
> one finds it. Sometimes it is like that, I do not know why. . . . Yes, it can
> annoy you! One has to pray, so that you will find the plants again rapidly!

Doña Flor also mentioned that she prayed as she looked for plants in the
woods. She informed me that there is a special prayer that is unspoken after
administering the medicine for snakebite that prevents the snake from returning to bite again. She learned how to deal with snakebite from her late
husband, whose specialty it was. Don Tomás mentioned something similar
from his childhood, suggesting a standardized ritual that may have been more
common in the past. Curers who treat snakebite exclusively are said to be
fairly common in Belize (Arvigo, personal communication, 1992).

Don Francisco allowed me to record the prayer he repeated when he
performed a *santiaguar* (blessing, sanctifying) ceremony for both me and
then for Don Tomás in turn. He invoked both Maya and Catholic deities
(mostly in Maya), asking humbly for their assistance in removing all evil winds
and enchantments from each of us. The Spanish words that he employed to
describe the variety of evils he was about to banish seemed old-fashioned
and liturgical: *maleficio* (curse, spell, witchcraft), *sortilegio* (sorcery, witchery).
The sensation of being in church was evoked by more than language; the
ceremony ended with his anointing us each with holy water, "so that our paths
would be clear."

Don Francisco stated that he uses different prayers when conducting
agricultural ceremonies, such as the rain-making *ch'a chaac*. Unfortunately, I
have not had the opportunity to witness such ceremonies and do not know
to what extent the prayers are standardized in ceremony or by the person
conducting it.

Bad luck with crops or human disease may be seen as the result of an
individual's personal behavior, such as forgetting to propitiate the gods. The
h-men takes therapeutic actions to address these problems as well as larger
imbalances between many human beings in a community and nature or the
gods, as in the case of the *ch'a chaac*. The agricultural ceremonies are
therapeutic in the same sense as the *santiaguar* and *kex* cleansing rituals; but
as public rather than private practices, these fall outside the scope of this book.

As I understand it, the *kex*, like many other Maya rituals, could be described as a type of spiritual bartering; ritual offerings including food are given in consideration of relieving a person's ill health or extreme personal hardship. I do not know what deities or entities are invoked, but Redfield and Villa Rojas (1962:174) say that "the *kex* is a promise of a return to be made to the winds if they abandon their victim, the patient." If the *santiaguar* does not bring the desired results, perhaps the more elaborate *kex* will.

Don Cósimo described a ceremony that is conducted once every two years by a *h-men* to protect himself from illnesses. If there are ten clients, each one brings a chicken. He will also need an *almud* (four kilos) of corn *masa* (dough made from ground corn, lime, and water), a half-kilo of ground *pepitas* (squash seeds), and a *garrafa* (five liters) of *aguardiente* (cane liquor) to share. The clients kill and prepare the chickens. The *masa* and the *pepitas* are made into *pibiwah* (special tortillas) and baked in a *pib*. The clients make a *mesa* (altar, table) in the form of an arch with branches of *habim* (a leguminous tree, *Piscidia piscipula,* figure 29) or *xiat* (a type of palm) branches. After the meal is served, the ceremony begins. As previously mentioned, Don Cósimo stated that each *h-men* has his own words, adding that some *h-mens* teach their students word for word, although he himself learned from dreams. Prayers appear to be highly individualized, although more formulaic prayers may be used in specific ceremonies. It seems logical that those who learn to cure from an elder may well model their prayers on those of their mentor.

Don Aldo emphasized the need to think positive thoughts when working with plants and plant medicines. He talks to his plants, encouraging them to grow, and believes that all living beings are connected by a flow of energy. In order to use plants to cure, he believes that you must have "good chemistry" connecting you to the plants: "I know you have to ask them, but I don't know how to. The *h-men,* what he does is ask the plant to cure you."

Whether deities are Maya, Catholic, or some combination thereof, it seems that the curers can communicate directly with them. They intercede with the supernaturals on behalf of patients and seek their guidance in the selection and location of suitable medicines. The *h-men* intercedes with supernaturals on behalf of both individual patients and entire communities in the case of agricultural ceremonies. His prayers are the only ones conducted in a public setting.

The emphasis on prayer among all the curers I have come to know has forced me to question any hierarchy that divides or categorizes curers on a basis of sacred versus profane practices. This division does not seem to exist in the minds of the curers I have come to know in Yucatan. Curing is at once a spiritual, magical, and empirical business.

Massage

What I have come to think of as "women's massage" is used by the two midwives included in my research, Doña Flor and Doña Francisca, in their treatment of female patients. Massage is used during the course of pregnancy to turn a breech position baby, if necessary, and to relieve discomfort in the mother's back and legs. The midwife may use massage to hasten delivery and utilizes it afterward to help reposition the mother's uterus. Massage and palpation of inner organs were used to diagnose my friend Mariela's medical problem.

Male practitioners dominate what I have come to think of as "chiropractic" massage. Don Pedro and Don Cósimo do this type of work. This form of treatment is applied to male and female patients, although I think that male patients may outnumber female patients simply because men's work in the *milpa* renders them more susceptible to these kinds of injuries. Several curers mentioned the existence of specialist bonesetters, although I have not met one. Redfield and Villa Rojas (1962:72,172) make a distinction between *kax baac* (bonesetter) and *ch'en zahi* (one who treats sprains and dislocations) stating that, although "a *kax baac* is strictly one who can set bones, the term is loosely used for those who know only *ch'en zahi*." This distinction continues today.

Massage therapy seems to be one of very few areas in Yucatecan curing that is gender specific. The fact that Yucatecan women are extremely modest may be a contributing factor; many prefer to be treated whenever possible by another woman. Although the majority of women now seem to prefer to give birth in a hospital setting because of perceived safety considerations, I have heard repeated complaints from women about the disregard for their personal modesty at the hospital. Traditionally, women even gave birth fully clothed, with the exception of their underclothes.

Plant Medicine

All the curers with whom I worked use plant medicine to a greater or lesser extent in their practices. None of them uses plant medicine exclusively, although it is usually the largest single component of their practices. Chapter 6 will examine the set of most commonly utilized plants and treatments. Here I limit myself to general comments on how the plants are used. Fresh plants (used whole or sometimes a specified part) are chopped fresh and applied as plasters to treat wounds, bruises, headaches, and skin irritations. The plasters may "draw" fevers or cause sores to come to a head. Fresh leaves may be crushed or coarsely chopped and their aroma and essential oils inhaled to stop nosebleeds or headaches. Plants are *sancochadas* (boiled) or *remojadas* (soaked or steeped), and either taken internally as teas or are used to bathe patients. Ratios of plant material to water are almost always specified. Sometimes sap, resin, or essential oil is applied directly to affected areas or taken internally. I have also seen tinctures for treatment of body aches and rheumatism prepared by soaking plant material in alcohol, which is rubbed onto the affected area.

Medicinal plants are usually gathered in the woods and fields as needed and used fresh, although two curers also dry and store plants. As stated, one curer has planted a supply of medicinals in his yard to have on hand. Plants may be used alone, combined with other plants, or in conjunction with pharmacy staples such as Vicks VapoRub, rubbing alcohol, and acetaminophen or kitchen items such as animal fat or coffee grounds. Several of the curers utilize more medicines composed of several plants than others, but the majority of plants are used as "simples."

Almost all the curers mentioned that although "natural medicine" was preferable and less expensive than other treatments, there were problems in its application. The problems most often noted are that some medicinals are only available in certain seasons, individual plants can be more or less potent, making consistent dosage a problem, and lastly, many older people complained that Yucatan "has been burned," meaning that the combination of population expansion and slash-and-burn agriculture has reduced the noncultivated plant resources.

Plant medicine is utilized empirically for treating symptoms of natural illnesses and for "unnatural" illnesses caused by magic. Sickness may be "sent" by other people, or it may be the result of encounters with evil winds or evil eye. These and other traditional concepts of disease will be discussed at length in the next chapter in relation to their treatments. The distinction made here between plant medicine and plant magic is a wholly artificial one, employed for organizational purposes only.

Plant Magic

Many prescriptions are obvious examples of the Doctrine of Signatures, or the concept of "like cures like." For example, a sinuous root that resembles a snake provides a cure for snakebite, or a yellow flower is used to treat jaundice. This concept is well known from medieval European herbals and may have been exported to Yucatan during the colonial period, although it could equally well be an example of the convergence that often occurs between European and Mayan traditions. It is also the basis of modern homeopathic treatments.

Plants not only cure diseases; they also prevent them. There are a number of plants that are commonly planted in houseyards, preferably at all four corners, in order to provide magical protection from evil winds, evil eye, and witchcraft. They include plants of European origin such as rue *(Ruta chalapensis)* and basil *(Ocimum* species), as well as native plants such as *sip che (Bunchosia* species) and *yax halal che (Pedilanthus itzaeus)*. Planting at each of the cardinal directions recreates a microcosm of the Maya universe, which is similarly bounded. Household gardens often contain numerous edible species that, as will be seen in the next chapter, are multiuse resources. Conducting a yard-by-yard survey to explore the prevalence of this group of plants in a given town would be a useful project, one I intend to pursue in the future.

Other plants that serve preventative functions include several species of *Cissus,* which are hung over doorways to prevent the entrance of witches in human or animal form. Witches can "suck your blood" while you sleep. Suspending the leaves of *Annona glabra* above doorways prevents the entrance of infections that come from exposure to corpses. These infections are transmitted to any family members who have open wounds and are a particular danger to women who have recently given birth to a child.

Protective plants are also placed under, over, or around sleeping hammocks. These include the bright red seeds of *achiote* or *annatto (Bixa orellana),* which are said to disperse measles; pieces of *Zanthoxylum* wood, which keep evil winds away; and *Ficus* leaves, which stop snoring. The cut-up pads of *Nopalea* cacti are arranged in the shape of five crosses and then placed around the hammock (again, at the four corners, with the fifth suspended over the center of the hammock) of a crying child to quiet and calm him or her.

Branches or sprigs of *Bunchosia* are used in rituals that cleanse the patient of a variety of ills, such as any lingering winds that may have "stuck" after attending agricultural ceremonies in the fields, evil eye, or bad luck. The patient receives a symbolic bath (which does not involve water at all) in which the curer brushes the patient from head to toe with the leaves of the *sip che* plant. The curer makes a series of crosses with each pass of the leaves as he (she?) moves down the patient's body. The movements are accompanied by silent or verbal prayers.

The best day to perform a *limpio* is Friday, because that is the day that the guardians of the plant are asleep. These guardians are *aluxes,* mischievous and at times vengeful miniature people who inhabit the woods, particularly around ruins, and are described as the assistants of the *balams.* This belief appears to be linked to the traditional idea that Tuesdays and Fridays are the best for curing. Tuesdays and Fridays may be good for curing, but roaming around the streets after midnight on those days is considered dangerous, a time when evil winds are out and about.

The *santiaguar* ritual described earlier in this chapter requires *sip che* branches to sweep the patient, who is then anointed with holy water on the head, chest, hands, and feet. A new set of branches is cut and used each time the ritual is performed, as though they "absorb" or draw off the evil influences from the patient's body. It is my impression that a *yerbatero(a)* may perform the *limpio,* whereas a *h-men* performs the *santiaguar* and *kex.*

While attending the feast day of the Virgin of the Immaculate Conception at the huge yellow cathedral at Izamal, I watched as devout visitors carried branches of *ruda (Ruta chalapensis)* around to each statue inside the church. The visitors would kiss the plant, then touch it gently to the image in front of them. This action was repeated at each station until the main image of the Virgin was reached, where two men (sacristans?) took the sprigs or branches from each person, touched the statue's feet, and placed the sprigs behind her. I have not learned the significance of this action, which may well have roots in medieval Spanish traditions.

It has become a truism that Maya people are often bilingual when it comes to religion as well as language. Several of the curers with whom I have worked make no distinction between Maya and Catholic deities when it comes to invoking supernatural assistance; the Holy Trinity, saints, *balams,* and a bewildering number of Virgins are all asked for help in curing. Elements of rituals from both religions are freely incorporated in curing practices. I do not know if this is the case for the agricultural ceremonies.

When one treats a child for evil eye, which manifests itself as fever or diarrhea, certain plants "sweep" the illness away from the patient. The leaves of the *cocuite* (possibly *Gliricidia sepium*) are used to anoint the baby with drops of water. Other plants, such as *Salvia coccinea* and *Blechum pyramidatum,* are boiled, cooled, and then the resulting medicine is used for bathing or washing the child.

Necklaces made from the poisonous but beautiful *oxoh (Abrus precatorius,* figure 1) seeds are worn as a charm to prevent attacks of *ojo.* The seeds are red with a black tip, suggesting an eye with its contrasting iris. Dr. Victoria Bricker noted that in colonial Spanish, *ojo* may have been pronounced *oxo,* suggesting a form of linguistic homeopathy. Amulets worn around the neck may contain pieces of branches from *Zanthoxylum,* which protect the wearer from evil winds. Roys (1931:309) mentions that the seeds of the *jaboncillo* or soap-berry *(Sapindus saponaria)* are used for making necklaces and rosaries. There are almost certainly other plants that are worn as *contras* (preventatives), and I have heard reference made to protective necklaces made from animal (jaguar) teeth as well. Stones found inside animals' bodies are considered lucky, like the bezoar stones of European traditions. The animal's power is said to come from the stone. That power is transferred to the person who possesses the stone, but only if it is kept secret; showing the stone to anyone causes it to lose its power. The stones may come from deer, wild boar, *tepezcuintli,* or wild turkey, but a stone from a jaguar is best.

Crystals

Previously I discussed the two basic patterns by which the curers in this research learned their skills. The two male curers who learned involuntarily, through dreams, also received a crystal or crystals from the *balams*. The crystals are the means by which the curer communicates with the *balams* and signal the owner's connection to them. As outlined earlier in this chapter, the crystals are used in many ways, primarily to help diagnose illnesses and in public agricultural ceremonies. Crystals are also used by at least one curer I know to *sacar la suerte* (tell fortunes).

In 1992 I paid to have my fortune told. I was seated across a small table from Don Cósimo. He lit a candle and placed three crystals in front of it. He intoned a prayer, which began as an audible plea in Spanish addressed to God, the Son, the Holy Ghost, and a number of saints, and then dropped to a rapid-fire whisper of what to me was unintelligible Maya. He picked up each crystal in turn, rubbed it, held it near the candle, and then told me the same fortune he had read for me using a deck of tarot cards. Like any good fortune-teller, Don Cósimo essentially told me what he knew I wanted to hear: that I would make many trips to Yucatan, enjoy good health, and so forth. This fortune-telling enterprise struck me as merely a sideline to his practice as a healer.

During an interview with Don Tomás, he explained to me how two curers could work together with their crystals in difficult cases. Years ago, his one-year-old niece had been lost. Two *h-mens* "joined forces" in order to rescue her. They prayed all night, working with their crystals. Then they told Don Tomás' father where to look for the little girl. She was found exactly where they said she would be, three kilometers away from her home sheltered in a cave, on the third day of the search. Caves are the territory of the *balams*.

Although curers may work together to increase their powers, the crystals themselves are not passed on from one generation of curers to another, although the power to cure may be. Don Tomás explained:

> We say that a person with a crystal, when he gets old, he talks with the *balams* about who to give his power to before he dies, to take the power before he dies and give it to his *semejante* (fellow man) . . . but there are some people who do not want to recommend their nephew or whoever, and when they die the culture dies too, disappears.

Dreams

The curers with whom I have worked respect dreams. Not only are dreams a major means of communication between human beings and supernaturals, but their meanings are often specific and predictive. If one dreams of a bull, it signifies death. A pig signifies a quarrel. A horse signifies rain, and a female donkey signifies drought. If a snake bites you, but you feel no pain, there will be a death in the house of another. If it bites and it hurts, the death will occur in your house. Redfield and Villa Rojas (1962:210–11) note some similar omens or predictions: even seeing snakes was a bad sign in Chan Kom, and dreams of many pigs or cats indicated the advent of a fight. Steggerda (1941:58–59) also recorded similar interpretations: Black bulls signified death, snakes were a sign of up-coming quarrels, and white horses fighting foretold the advent of rain. Several of my own dreams were interpreted as a sign that I wanted to cure. Colors in dreams are said to have specific meanings as well: white = peace, blue = dependence, red = valor.

Other Practices: Obsolete?

Despite references to the use of bleeding or cupping in the literature (Redfield and Villa Rojas 1962:162–64) and the field, none of the curers I know utilize these techniques. Divination using kernels of corn was recorded by Villa Rojas (1945:133) for Quintana Roo, by Redfield and Villa Rojas (1962:170) for Yucatan between 1930 and 1940, and by Evon Vogt (1976:94–96) for highland Chiapas, although I have not heard of this practice at all. Barbara Tedlock (1982:60) mentions the use of divining seeds (of *Erythrina corallodendron*) and crystals among the Quiché for highland Guatemala.

Several curers told me about non-Maya practitioners who used eggs in their practices in Yucatan. Either an egg was placed beneath the patient's bed or hammock to "absorb" any evil influences, or the egg was broken into a glass of water, and the curer "read" the forms of the egg to diagnose illnesses. In *Chicano Folk Medicine from Los Angeles, California*, author Roeder (1988:242–43) mentions similar uses of eggs among Mexican-American curers in the United States, noting that eggs are used in the diagnosis and treatment of evil eye, in a ritual said to be of Spanish origin.

Western Medicine

Each of the curers I have come to know utilizes differential amounts of Western medicine. Don Aldo, of course, has had extensive Western medical training. His experiments have convinced him that the synergistic effects of certain Western and Maya treatments are often more effective than either treatment alone; for example, he treats fevers with a combination of aspirin and either *chacah* (*Bursera simaruba*, figure 8) or *zacate limón* (*Cymbopogon citratus*, figure 20). He believes that herbal medicines usually have fewer side effects than do Western medicines.

Doña Flor has had some training in Western obstetrical and gynecological procedures. She is convinced of the efficacy of antibiotics in treating infections and refers patients to Dr. Estrella when she judges prescription medicine to be necessary. All the others with whom I worked incorporate Western medicines in various forms into their practices. I do not see these introductions as heralding the demise of traditional curing in Yucatan; rather, I think it highlights the flexibility of the curers. Their ability to incorporate new elements and practices attests to the ongoing viability of traditional curing in Yucatan.

Over-the-counter drugs from the pharmacy are utilized in conjunction with traditional treatments. Where one curer uses either coffee or hearth ashes to apply the leaves of *Ricinus communis* (figure 31) to a patient's chest to draw fever and congestion, his colleague may use Vicks VapoRub® instead. Wood from the *tan caz che* tree (*Zanthoxylum* sp.) is soaked in rubbing alcohol to make a treatment for arthritis. Alcohol is added to a tea made with the bark of the sea grape *(Coccoloba uvifera)* and taken for ulcers. Aspirin and acetaminophen are highly regarded as febrifuges, although these drugs are sometimes prohibitively expensive in Yucatan. If available, a tablet may also be applied to a sore tooth for pain relief. Aspirin is considered to be a potent drug: several women friends were shocked that I would take it for the relief of mild menstrual cramps. Vitamin tablets are likewise regarded as "very strong" medicine.

Conclusion

The categories of curers mentioned in Redfield and Villa Rojas (1962:75) still exist. The words used to refer to those categories have undergone some change in the past sixty years; the terms *dzadzac* and *x-dzadzac* are being replaced by the Spanish *yerbatero(a)*, although they are still understood, at least by older people and curers. I did not hear anyone use the Maya terms for midwife. The Spanish *partera* and *sobadora* are both used, although *comadrona* was not. Two Maya terms, *utzkil a bac* and *kax baac,* were used, along with the Spanish *sobador,* when discussing masseurs and bonesetters. The distinction between these specialties suggested by Roys (1931:xxii–xxiii) still exists.

The overlap and distinctions among all the types of practices has been discussed at length. Although an idealized model with clear-cut categories has been presented to me by the curers themselves, in reality the different "specialties" are more realistically seen as overlapping components, which each curer combines in a unique way. The concept of a hierarchy appears to have been imposed from outside the culture in which the curers live. All of the curers discussed here emphasize the importance of prayer, faith, and positive thought in their practices. Spirituality is always an important component.

The negative roles of witch and sorcerer may be considered the dark or flip side of the curing practice as a whole; the power to do that kind of work is said to be purchased with the soul of the curer. Although my data on the subject are limited, I hypothesize that the roles of witch and sorcerer may have once been more sharply distinguished. It is interesting that a woman may not be a sorcerer, although women witches are feared and considered powerful.

The roles of the midwife and the masseur appear to be at least partially gender specific or complementary. The ambiguity concerning the gender specificity of the role of *h-men* indicates that things may be changing. The female *x-men* may be a relatively recent innovation, or perhaps the term is just being used in a general way to indicate a female curing practitioner. The use of crystals among women may be more acceptable than it once was, perhaps by default. The trend toward commuting, especially among men, to a job located some distance from a home town or village may have contributed to this situation. The agricultural and priestly aspects of the *h-men*'s office may be the only (last?) areas forbidden to women. The question of whether women must borrow or share the power of the crystals that male supernaturals bestow on men would bear further inquiry. Men receive the crystals at what is considered the age of maturity in the forest, far from home and the woman's traditional sphere of influence.

CHAPTER SIX

Common Treatments and Traditional Concepts of Disease and Its Cause

This chapter begins by considering the plants listed in table 1 (starting on p. 71) that I believe to be among the most commonly utilized species in Yucatan today. Only those plants that were used in the same way by more than one curer are included. The table lists those species that I collected more than once with different curers, plants that were collected once and then later orally verified or augmented by a second curer, and two common citrus species not supported by voucher specimens.

I collected plants with three of the curers: Don Tomás, Don Pedro, and Don Cósimo. The three did not consistently examine or comment on each other's uses as recorded in my field notes, but conversations took place about what I had learned from each curer. Plants and what they cure were discussed during walks, at meals, and so forth. Thus, the number of plants presented probably represents only a portion of the most commonly utilized species.

The curers of the peninsula, with their specialized knowledge of local plants, have employed a very similar set of plants for medicinal and other uses for many years. The curers almost always know the plants by the same common name. The uses are more variable, but basically the same set of plants is utilized. The final section of this chapter focuses on diagnosis and treatment of "culture-bound" diseases such as evil eye, evil winds, *bilis,* and *pasmo.*

It is clear from table 1 that edible plants are among the most versatile species, often being used in several ways. They are common species and therefore accessible. Medicinal and edible resources are often no farther away than one's own *solar.* The sap or resin of the *ramón (Brosimum alicastrum)* is a well-known treatment for coughs, the fruit makes a delicious filling for pastry, and the leaves of the plant have been used for animal fodder for a long time. Guava *(Psidium guajava)* leaves and fruit are used to treat diarrhea and skin complaints. Papaya *(Carica papaya)* sap or resin is used for a range of skin complaints, including snakebite. The fruit aids digestion and is a laxative (along with the seeds) when eaten in quantity. Avocado *(Persea americana)* fruit is used for skin beautification, the bark is a treatment for rheumatism, and its leaves are used to treat diarrhea. The seed may be grated and used as a condiment in cooking sauces.

The sap from *chaya* (*Cnidoscolus chayamansa*, figure 16) leaves is taken as a purgative, and the edible leaves may also be used to make a tea, which is taken as a general tonic. Lime *(Citrus aurantifolia)* fruit is baked in hearth ashes and applied as a skin treatment, and its juice is used as a tonic for the libido and as an antidote to poison. Sour orange *(Citrus aurantium)* juice is a treatment for *bilis*, scrapings of the peel are a remedy for bruises, and a tea made from the leaves is taken for vomiting and to increase appetite.

Many nonedible species have multiple uses as well. The roots of several *Zanthoxylum* species are scraped and soaked in alcohol to make a rubbing compound used to alleviate the pain of rheumatism. Pieces of its wood are carried in *sabucam* (bags traditionally made from henequen fiber, now also increasingly made of plastic) or placed beneath hammocks to provide protection against evil winds. The leaves of the *habin* tree (*Piscidia piscipula*, figure 29) are used as a remedy for coughs, and its branches are widely utilized in the construction of *mesas* in traditional Maya ceremonies. The wood is also used in house construction. The bark of the *chacah*, or gumbo limbo tree (*Bursera simaruba*, figure 8), is used in treating fevers and snakebite, and the leaves are used for other skin complaints, including allergic reactions to *Metopium brownei*. The aromatic oils of cedar *(Cedrela mexicana)* are inhaled to stop nosebleeds and are applied to earaches. The wood is prized for house and furniture construction. *Bauhinia divaricata* (figure 5) leaves are used in a tea taken for control of diabetes and are a remedy for sore throat "when blood comes up." The root is made into a laxative tea for children. The seeds of the wild basil, *Ocimum micranthum*, are used as a remedy for eye complaints, and its leaves are utilized in treatments for pimples and dysentery. The leaves of *Cecropia peltata* are smokeable and are also made into a tea used to treat diabetes. The hollow stems may be used as irrigation pipes.

Many of the most valuable species of plants are common rather than exotic or rare and as such are readily available resources. Many of them lend themselves to cultivation and so may be suitable subjects for projects dealing with renewable resources. Appendix A contains a complete listing of uses recorded for all plants in my collection.

The Hot/Cold Dichotomy, Evil Eye, Evil Winds, Bilis, and Pasmo: Diagnosis and Treatment

No study of common treatments employed by curers in Yucatan would be complete without discussing what are known as "folk" or "culture-bound" diseases, such as *bilis*, *pasmo*, evil eye, and evil winds. Understanding the treatment of these conditions also entails some description of common theories of disease causation.

Sickness may result from natural causes (including germs), emotional upsets, witchcraft, neglect of the gods or other supernaturals, hot/cold imbalances, or from encounters with disease-causing agents such as evil winds, certain birds, and persons who have evil eye. Appropriate treatments may include "empirical" remedies for specific symptoms, ritual actions, or some combination of both sorts of therapies. In the previous chapter, the problem of overlap was discussed in relation to the roles of curers in Yucatan. Likewise, traditional concepts of disease and its diagnosis and treatment tend to overlap and blend into one another.

My hypothesis is that curers in Yucatan believe that disruption of harmony or natural balance creates disease or increases vulnerability to it. This concept of balance underlies the "folk" conditions in this chapter and guides their treatment. Both an internal balance and harmony among an individual, his or her family, and the natural and supernatural environment are necessary to good health. Good health is the steady-state, or normal situation, which is punctuated by illness or misfortune. The concept of a healthful balance may well have been present in both Yucatecan and Spanish cultures prior to their confrontation in the sixteenth century. If so, the convergence of the concept in the two cultures, which merged to produce that of present-day Yucatan, would help to explain its widespread distribution.

Ignoring or forgetting one's obligations to the old Maya gods of the fields or other supernaturals creates one kind of imbalance, which is manifested in either sickness or bad luck in agricultural endeavors. These imbalances may be corrected with the help of a *h-men* or by simply making appropriate offerings without an intermediary. According to Yucatec Maya tradition, a righteous person should theoretically also be a healthy person. But in reality, bad things do happen to good people, and other explanations exist for such occurrences.

Some health problems, such as *bilis* and *pasmo,* are related to strong or excessive emotions. These (respectively) "hot" and "cold" conditions are imbalances that are treated with medicines of the opposite intrinsic quality; if one has a "hot" condition, "cold" treatments will be prescribed to reinstate a healthy balance, and vice versa.

Evil winds and evil eye may be seen as conditions that are brought on by encounters or contact between persons or forces of unequal strength or power. In the case of the first condition, human and supernatural entities collide, and the weaker human being becomes ill as a result. In the case of evil eye, the encounter is between human beings of differential strength: an adult and a child. The damage may be caused inadvertently in both conditions, or the winds may "stick" to a person because of some proscribed behavior, such as illicit lovemaking out in the bush, the territory of the *balams.*

Many Yucatecans are familiar with the conditions of evil eye, evil winds, *bilis,* and *pasmo* and make distinctions based on the hot/cold dichotomy, but this is not to say that they are all components with discrete roles in an all-encompassing system. As Redfield and Villa Rojas (1962:161) pointed out in their chapter on sickness and its cure in Chan Kom:

> It would be a misrepresentation to assert any detailed consistency or system or rules governing native thinking on these matters. All that can be done is to state the ideas that are paramount and indicate some of the extensions of these ideas into various classes of situations.

The state of present-day knowledge of these topics is even more fragmentary than in the days of Redfield and Villa Rojas. The information I recorded is generally similar to that which appears in *Chan Kom: A Maya Village* (Redfield and Villa Rojas 1962) and in Redfield (1941), *The Folk Culture of Yucatan,* except that mine is even less complete.

Yucatecan treatments for the above-mentioned conditions may be different from those utilized in other Mexican states, but the conditions themselves are neither limited to the peninsula nor to Maya cultures. Variations on these themes are known throughout the Americas; therefore, the term "culture-bound disease" seems inaccurate, unless one takes the unlikely view that they are of wholly Spanish origin and are to be found unaltered in all areas colonized by Spain.

I have already suggested that all of the above-named conditions may be seen as either the cause or the effect of various imbalances. They are sometimes diagnosed by a process of elimination. When all else fails to explain a sickness or run of misfortunes, these old stand-bys are always available. Once diagnosed, a familiar course of treatment is prescribed to deal with the problem. Diagnosis and treatment of these conditions provides a culturally intelligible explanation for what may have otherwise been inexplicable, and a course of action one can undertake to stop problems encountered in daily life. Order may be imposed upon chaos.

The term "folk diseases" is laden with connotations suggesting something whimsical, quaint, or at any rate not serious. In our culture, the symptoms of some of these conditions might suggest very real mental health problems, such as depression and anxiety. Their treatment may provide psychological relief to those suffering from them. Mental or emotional states result from physical states and vice versa. Perhaps the term "folk diseases" merely implies that the conditions are more prevalent in rural areas than in big cities and among poor people rather than rich ones. Although I have not conducted research to support this hypothesis, I suspect that it is true. Older people may perceive the above conditions to be more of a threat than the younger generations and are more likely to take precautions against them. Younger people may be more skeptical, discounting their elders' views as "superstitions."

Here I approach these topics from the perspective of diagnosis and common treatment. Treatments remain relatively standard, and means of diagnosis illuminate the differences and similarities between diseases and conditions. One thing is consistently said of all of them; only curers can provide relief from them, not (Western) doctors.

The Hot/Cold Dichotomy

The hot/cold dichotomy applies to more than just diseases. Treatment of these diseases involves foodstuffs that are also assigned hot/cold values. For example, honey is hot, and limes are cold. A few of the curers with whom I have worked also classify a few plants and animals as being more or less hot or cold. Hot and cold usually refer to intrinsic characteristics rather than degrees of temperature, although physical temperature also comes into play in terms of disease causation and treatment. Hot treatments remedy cold conditions and vice versa. Imbalances create problems.

Most scholars agree that the hot/cold dichotomy is probably a remnant of the larger four-part humoral system that was imported, at least in simplified form, to Yucatan from Greece or Persia via Spain (see, for example, George Foster's [1994] *Hippocrates' Latin American Legacy: Humoral Medicine in the New World* for a full treatment of the subject and Beatrice Roeder's [1988] *Chicano Folk Medicine from Los Angeles, California* for a succinct discussion of the hot/cold concept). According to the (Galenic) humoral system, everything in the universe is composed of varying quantities of four elements, hot/cold and dry/moist. The hot/cold dichotomy seems to have eclipsed that of dry/ moist sometime after it arrived in the New World, as the former concept is widespread in Latin America and the latter nonexistent.

In my experience it has been the exception, rather than the rule, when curers have spontaneously identified plants as "hot" or "cold." Many frustrating interviews were spent trying to uncover the extent of this system of classification. I can only state with certainty that plants that grow near *cenotes* (sinkholes) are considered to be "cold" or "fresh." "Cold" plants such as *habin* (*Piscidia piscipula*, figure 29) and *sip che* (*Bunchosia swartziana)* are important elements of traditional Maya ceremonies. The kapok tree (*Ceiba aesculifolia*, figures 14 and 15), another "cold" plant, is symbolically important in Maya cosmology. Today most conditions and treatments are unrelated to this dichotomy.

People do talk about having either "hot" or "cold" blood and "hot" or "cold" hands. People are born with one or the other and are thus more or less suited for different occupations. For example, people with "cold" hands are not good cooks. If they prepare beans, it will take a very long time for them to finish cooking. People with "hot" blood are strong, large, and work hard. They are attracted to others with "hot" blood, and the same is true for "cold" blooded people. And this is how it should be: "mixed" marriages might be detrimental to the health of one or both of the partners. Bonding of opposites apparently does not create a new balance. Redfield and Villa Rojas (1962:163) recorded very similar, but much more detailed information in Chan Kom. Villa Rojas (1945:133) describes similar beliefs among the Maya of Quintana Roo. In that state, people with "hot hands" are said to be the most likely carriers of evil eye. At least one curer I know has correlated this traditional concept to that of modern blood types. Type B blood, for example, which I have, is "hot." Type O, the universal donor, is neutral. An individual's blood and hands may be predicative of physical characteristics and perhaps of propensity toward certain diseases as well. *Bilis* and *pasmo* are linked to the hot/cold dichotomy. Whether they are cause or effect is hard to say.

Bilis

Bilis literally means "bile," or "biliousness." In Anglo-Saxon North America, we know that bile is a substance secreted by the liver that aids in the digestion of lipids. In Yucatan, as in other parts of Mexico (and probably Latin America), it is also a condition brought on by an excess of strong emotions, especially anger. Anger is a "hot" emotion, and it creates an imbalance in the body of the person who experiences it. "Cold" therapy is required to correct it. In *Chicano Folk Medicine from Los Angeles, California,* Roeder (1988:318) states that, "*Bilis* may be the single most widespread condition in Mexico."

How does one diagnose the disease? The symptoms appear after an emotional upset and may include continued irritability or "nerves." Anger or emotional upset triggers the production of bile, which in turn causes stomach problems and more agitation. Treatments break the cycle, restoring mental equilibrium and reducing the production of bile in the liver (some say that bile is produced by the spleen).

Several curers prescribe orange juice for treating *bilis.* The patient must drink the juice each morning before breakfast to cure the problem. Variations include heating the juice and adding water and salt to it. Anger and emotional upset are "hot" conditions. By taking orange juice, a "half-cold" or "cold" drink (regardless of its physical temperature), the patient's mental and physical balance is restored. It may be soothing to a person who has recently suffered an upsetting experience to know that something is being done to ameliorate their situation.

Harmony, tranquility, and balance are desirable in all aspects of life and are necessary for maintaining good health. When a friend found me crying in what I thought was a private spot, he tried to calm me down, explaining that I would make myself ill if I continued. The connection between mind and body is strong; crying would result in physical illness. It is interesting to note the increasing extent to which doctors in this country are now acknowledging the effects of mental conditions, such as stress, on their patients' bodies.

Pasmo

If *bilis* is a "hot" condition, *pasmo* may be seen as its opposite. *Pasmo* literally means a chill and can also refer to diverse "cold" conditions such as tetanus, eye-twitching and convulsions, infertility in women, and postpartum diseases. I was told that this condition, like *bilis*, is more likely to affect adults than children. Don Cósimo described it like this: "You get it when you are older, after giving birth, or bathing; if you drink water or something cold and then you begin to sweat and lose strength, that is *pasmo.*" Other people said that you could get it if you were very warm, resting under a blanket in your hammock, and then put your feet on a cold floor. *Pasmo* seems to have a more direct relation to actual, physical temperatures than *bilis.* I was repeatedly warned about the dangers of drinking "cold" drinks after a hot and tiring plant-collecting trip and was advised to cool off a bit before taking a cold shower, presumably because the change in physical temperature would be too great and therefore unhealthful.

Redfield and Villa Rojas (1962:161–62) note that in Chan Kom, eating too many "cold" foods, especially when one is overheated from work, may produce weakness and sterility. They state that "any weakness, anemia, loss of appetite or low physical condition, especially in a woman" may be considered to be *pasmo.* As I understand it, the condition may also be the result of a fright or shock and is not limited to women; a man in Pisté was said to be suffering from *pasmo* after falling off the roof of a house he was in the process of building.

I recorded most of my information about *pasmo* during plant-collecting trips. *Morinda yucatanensis, Melochia pyramidata,* and *Rivina humilis* were mentioned repeatedly in connection with its treatment. *Rivina humilis* is used to cure an ailment called *síis* (cold). I was told by one curer that this was an *enfermedad del frío* (a cold sickness) that is contracted "when you wake up hot and go out into a cool wind." *Síis* resembles *pasmo* and may in fact be the Maya name for the latter illness. Interestingly, a wind is the agent that brings on the condition.

Evil Winds

Redfield (1941:305) stressed the importance of evil winds in conceptions of disease in Yucatan. His definition of them has been helpful to my understanding of these entities. He says:

> These are in part associated with actual movements of air, in part regarded as malevolent supernatural beings, and in part considered as groups of symptoms making up diseases. The concept exists both in generalized form, "wind," and as many separately distinguished and often semipersonified "winds." They are connected with wells, caves, and water generally.

The connection between *balams* and caves has been previously noted: in the last chapter I related the story of how the little lost girl was found "sheltered" in a cave, after the two *h-mens* worked together with their crystals to locate her. The cave was hardly a place a toddler of a year and a half or so could have reached without supernatural intervention. Caves are traditionally seen as entrances to the underworld and therefore as logical points of connection to supernatural beings in Maya and many other Mesoamerican cultures (Covarrubias 1957:57–58). In *The Blood of Kings,* authors Linda Schele and Mary Ellen Miller (1986:42) state that the Maya universe was composed of three levels: the Overworld, the Middleworld, and the Underworld. The last-mentioned level was entered "either through a cave or through bodies of standing water, such as the ocean or a lake."

Balams (and sometimes their helpers, the *aluxes*) are said to "carry" winds. This negative attribute reflects the ambiguous relationship between these supernaturals and human beings. *Balams* may watch over villages, teach curers how to cure, and guard lost children (who may be returned as changelings), but they are dangerous forces that must be respected and propitiated. They may be helpful to mankind if they are so inclined, but their very presence may be marked, or better said, accompanied, by harmful forces.

How does one diagnose evil winds? The answers seemed clear:

> When you have been in a cave, when you feel a bad headache, like you have drunk too much, but you haven't had anything to drink, and you vomit; or if you are shaking, and your mouth and head are moving, and you fall down on the ground.

A great many individual winds are noted by both Redfield (1941:118, 305) and Redfield and Villa Rojas (1962:166–67). The authors recorded that contact with them brings on the same kind of symptoms described above.

One of the first plants that Don Tomás showed me was *sip che (Bunchosia swartziana).* He explained that this "plant of the *balams*" was used to get rid of evil winds and their effects. Only a *curandero* (curing practitioner) or a *h-men* could enact the cure. On another plant-collecting trip, Don Tomás told me that *sip che* was used after traditional Maya ceremonies to disperse both the *aluxes* and the evil winds. The ceremonies apparently create a supernaturally charged atmosphere, which must be normalized. Each person who attends should be "hit" or "swept" with leafy branches so that they will not be "bothered" by the winds or *aluxes.* Redfield and Villa Rojas (1962:165) noted similarities between certain winds and *aluxes,* along with the tendency of Chan Kom people to merge these entities.

Bunchosia swartziana was consistently mentioned as a treatment for evil winds. I believe it is the most commonly used plant in dispersing the winds or treating their effects. Pieces of the wood of *Zanthoxylum* species may also be carried or placed under hammocks as protection from evil winds. Several curers mentioned that planting certain plants in the corners of one's houseyard was another measure taken against them. *Pedilanthus itzaeus* was frequently mentioned. In addition to planting at the four corners, some curers suggested a fifth plant in the center and also burying a cross made from pieces of the plant's distinctive zigzag stem there.

Other plants, such as *Ocimum micranthum* and *Ruta chalapensis* are planted in houseyards to provide protection against evil eye or some combination of evil winds and evil eye. Although these conditions may have originated on opposite sides of the Atlantic Ocean, their fusion or blending, noted by Redfield and Villa Rojas (1962:168) in Chan Kom, continues today.

Evil Eye

The origin of the concept of evil eye is uncertain. As Roeder (1988:5–6) says,

> Belief in the evil eye is widespread from Scotland to Sri Lanka. The consensus of scholarly opinion is that this belief originated at an early time in the Near East and spread by diffusion in numerous directions and throughout several language stocks (Indo-European being but one of them), generally in association with peasant-urban and hierarchical societies, as opposed to nomadic or hunting cultures. It is associated with Christianity, Judaism, Hinduism, and ancient Zoroastrianism. Although it is possible that the Arabs brought belief in the evil eye to Spain, it is also possible that it was transmitted to Spain by Jews or Romans.

In Yucatan, evil eye can be given inadvertently to a child by an adult with just a glance. The giver is not an evil person, or a witch; they are simply born with the ability to give the condition to others. "It is just something that they do; they are not to blame" (Don Pedro). The person "with a strong glance" may have a mark of some kind near or between his eyes that signals his or her ability. It is most likely to happen if such a person is hot and thirsty from a journey and then looks at a child. Again, excess temperature causes a dangerous state. The smaller the child, the more susceptible they are thought to be. Power imbalances create a situation that may be dangerous to the weaker, smaller person, much as the presence of evil winds attendant upon supernaturals may injure human beings.

Evil eye usually manifests itself as crying or diarrhea (especially "green diarrhea") in children. One eye of an afflicted child may become visibly larger than the other. In less obvious cases, the diagnosis may be made by the process of elimination; as Don Cósimo put it, "when you have tried everything and a baby still cries and does not want to eat, then it must be *ojo*." The cure may be as simple as having the giver of the evil eye hug the child, or it may require further "baths" (with or without water) to make the child well if they are already exhibiting symptoms of the disease.

In other parts of Mexico, the damage is done by the glance of a person who envies the child or admires it to excess. In these areas, admiring adults may take preventative measures such as pinching the baby or making a disparaging remark after fondling it. More serious cases require the assistance of a curer. Eggs are frequently mentioned in connection with curing evil eye in Roeder's (1988) interviews with Mexican-Americans, along with herbs, including rue *(Ruta chalapensis)*. The physical resemblance between an egg and an eye may be important to the cure.

Wearing a necklace of *oxoh* (*Abrus precatorius,* figure 1) seeds, which resemble eyes, prevents evil eye. A cure may be effected by bathing the child in water with its leaves. *Diphysa carthagenensis* (figure 21) and *Salvia coccinea* are also used in similar baths. Less frequently, the treatment may be ingested. Don Cósimo described a mixture of four plants that should be taken internally for *ojo: epazote xiu* (not *epazote*), *hinojo, on xiu (om xiu?)*, and *cambal ojo.* The plants mentioned were dried and chopped after a trip to his *rancho* at Xkalakdzonot, and it was impossible to make voucher specimens of them.

The concept of evil eye and that of a special kind of wind called *Ojo de agua* (spring), also seem to have merged. Don Cósimo described it as "an evil wind that comes with the rains," which brings fever to nursing mothers or diarrhea to children. Earlier he had told me that evil eye does not bring fever but diarrhea. Two plants, *Ageratum conyzoides* and *Calliandra grisebachii* (figure 10), are taken internally to cure the condition.

In their discussion of evil winds Redfield and Villa Rojas (1962:164–65) mention that "the winds that blow from the water are the winds that are apt to bring sickness. In Yucatan, water appears in just three forms: the sea, the cenotes, and the rain. When winds come from any of these, they are evil winds." *Ojo-ik-ha* is the wind that "blows from the water just before the rain comes."

Redfield and Villa Rojas (1962:162) also mention a disease known as *holom-x-al*, which occurs in postpartum women and is caused by "taking too many cold things." The symptoms of the disease sound like *pasmo*: pallor, loss of appetite, menstrual irregularity, and the like. Hot remedies and hot foods are given to the patient, along with an herb called *holom-x-al*. *Holom x-al* is the common name I recorded for *Ageratum conyzoides*. This serves as an example of the degree to which traditional concepts merge with one another in present-day Yucatan. I hypothesize that the evil winds that come with the rain bring about a change of temperature that can cause ill effects in weak and vulnerable persons, such as new mothers and their babies.

Evil Birds

Certain birds are blamed for transmitting illness (usually a fever, but some-times incessant crying) to children. The birds do so by flying over the roofs of houses at night or by perching there. *Ak'ab' xiu* (*Blechum pyramidatum*, figure 6), a plant whose common name means "night herb," is boiled with water, cooled, and used to bathe children and so cure them of "night sweats."

The birds are either described as *bujos* (owls), or as large gray birds with yellow eyes, hoof-like feet, and red mouths. Villa Rojas (1945:135) recorded in-formation in Quintana Roo about an evil bird, called the *mesa-hol*, which is said to have flown "with its body upside down." The crying of owls and other nocturnal birds near a house is also a bad omen, announcing sickness or impending death. In his book of Zinacantecan dreams, *Of Wonders Wild and New*, Robert Laughlin (1976:19) records Romin Teratol's dream in which an owl calls out in the night. Teratol responds (in his dream) by going to find and kill the "messenger of death." In a footnote to the above dream, Laughlin mentions the following Mexican saying: *"Cuando canta el tecolote el indio muere."* (When a screech owl calls, the Indian dies.)

An illustration from the late colonial period Kaua manuscript (Latin American Library at Tulane University, Kaua, Chilam Balam de. Ms.) depicts another evil bird, a graphic depiction (or perhaps a symbol) of a disease called "Spider-snake-macaw-wind seizure." In Ralph Roys' (1965) translations of Maya medical incantations and prescriptions in *Ritual of the Bacabs*, the curers beg and exhort various personified diseases to leave the bodies of their patients. The patients may have taken comfort from their curers' familiarity with the problem afflicting them, which was demonstrated by the curer calling out the names of the personified disease's "parents," "trees," and "birds." Roys (1965:4) states that they are related to the name day of a person's (or disease's?) birth. The conception of a bird as either the carrier of a disease or a disease itself is an ancient one in Yucatan.

Other Common Treatments

The number nine is considered lucky in Yucatan. Nine is a magical number in both Christian and Maya mythology and medicine. Several magical treatments require that an action be repeated nine times. In the case of the remedy for *tuch* (a protruding belly-button), a section of *ha'as ak (Merremia dissecta)* is used to touch the patient's belly-button nine times as the sun is setting. The fruit of the *sutup (Helicteres barvensis)* is inserted in the mouth of a nonver-bal child and turned nine times to make them speak.

Nine is a number that is repeated in prescriptions. Nine leaves of the *habin* (*Piscidia piscipula*, figure 29) are used to treat a cough. Water in which nine of the ant larvae found living in the *subin (Acacia collinsii*, figure 2) have been washed is secretly given to a cuckolded man to drink so that he will "wake up" and realize his situation. Nine drops of resin from the *kik che* tree (*Apoplanesia paniculata,* figure 3) are taken in water to cure dysentery.

Steggerda (1941:54–64) likewise noted the significance of the number nine in treatments from around Pisté:

> The use of the number nine is common in the cure of diseases. Whooping cough may be prevented by hanging in the doorway on nine successive days as many gourds of pozole as there are members in the household. . . . Nine kernels of corn are ground and applied to granulated eyelids, and skin troubles may be cured with a concoction made by boiling together nine pieces of fish skin, nine pieces of corncob, and nine small pebbles.

Steggerda notes that the number nine is significant in both Maya cosmology and European cultures. As an example, he cites a fourth century A.D. medical prescription from Marcellus Empiricus, which calls for nine grains of barley to be touched individually to a sty to cure it. Simultaneously reciting a "magical formula in Greek" completed the cure.

The bark of the *kik che* tree is also used in a treatment that provides an example of the so-called Doctrine of Signatures, or the concept of like-cures-like. When the bark is boiled with water, it produces a red medicine that the patient sits in to treat hemorrhoids. In Roys' (1934:xxi) introduction to *The Ethno-Botany of the Maya,* the author notes that in the colonial sources he examined, including the first volume of the Kaua manuscript (Latin American Library at Tulane University, Kaua, Chilam Balam de. Ms.),

> Certain vines thought to resemble a snake were considered a cure for snake-bite. Yellow plants or fruits were given for jaundice and biliousness, and red plants or fruits were considered efficacious for diseases characterized by vomiting blood and dysentery.

True to this tradition, I was told that ingesting the snake-like root of the *contrahierba* plant (undetermined species) was a remedy for snakebite and that the red seeds of the *achiote (Bixa orellana)* could cure the red eruptions characteristic of measles. The black and red seeds of the *oxoh (Abrus precatorius,* figure 1) resemble eyes and may prevent evil eye in the same manner as eye-shaped glass beads worn in Turkey today.

Roys' finding that the majority of the Maya medical texts contain symptom-oriented prescriptions "based on objective observations of the effects of certain plants on the human system" still characterizes the vast majority of treatments used by curers today. Table 1 follows.

TABLE 1
Common Treatments and Uses

*The first column lists the category of use; the second contains
the scientific names of the plants employed, in alphabetical order.*

Use	Plants
Bilis	Several species of orange, especially *Citrus aurantium* (Christm.) Swingle
Cigarettes *Sida acuta* is said to be "like marijuana,"whereas *Cecropia peltata* and the *Piper* species are "like tobacco."	*Cecropia peltata* L. *Piper* sp. *Sida acuta* Burm. (figure 32)
Colds	*Annona squamosa* L. *Cydista potosina* (Schum. & Loes.) Loes. figure 19)
Coughs, sore throat	*Bauhinia divaricata* L. (figure 5) *Brosimum alicastrum* Swartz *Gossypium hirsutum* L. *Piscidia piscipula* (L.) Sargent *Sida acuta* Burm. (figure 32)
Crying in children See also **Ojo**	*Cassia stenocarpa* Vogel (figure 11) *Nopalea* sp.
Diuretics: treatment of diabetes, retention of urine, passing stones	*Bauhinia divaricata* L. (figure 5) *Cecropia peltata* L. *Cnidoscolus chayamansa* McVaugh (figure 16) *Euphorbia hypericifolia* L. *Jatropha gaumeri* Greenman (figure 25) *Malmea depressa* (Baillon) Fries *Tecoma stans* (L.) Kunth
Earache	*Cedrela mexicana* M. Roem.
Edible fruits, seeds, or leaves All species have at least one other use. *Lonchocarpus longistylus* (figure 26) and *Bromelia pinguin* (figure 7) are used to make alcoholic drinks and are so included with the edibles.	*Annona squamosa* L. *Bixa orellana* L. *Bromelia pinguin* L. (figure 7) *Brosimum alicastrum* Swartz *Byrsonima crassifolia* (L.) Kunth *Carica papaya* L. *Citrus aurantifolia* L. *Citrus aurantium* (Christm.) Swingle *Cnidoscolus chayamansa* McVaugh (figure 16) *Cordia dodecandra* A.DC. *Lonchocarpus longistylus* Pittier (figure 26) *Persea americana* Miller *Psidium guajava* L.

TABLE 1 cont'd

Use	Plants
Eye complaints	*Erythrina standleyana* Krukoff *Ocimum micranthum* Willd. *Spermacoce* sp.
Fever	*Blechum pyramidatum* (Juss.) Urban (figure 6) *Bursera simaruba* (L.) Sargent (figure 8) *Casimiroa tetrameria* Millsp. *Ricinus communis* L. (figure 31)
Headache	*Crataeva tapia* L. (figure 18) *Piper* sp. *Plantago major* L. (figure 30) *Zanthoxylum* sp.
Nosebleeds	*Cassia atomaria* L. *Cedrela mexicana* M. Roem. *Borreria pulchra* Millsp.
Ojo	*Abrus precatorius* L. (figure 1) *Ageratum conyzoides* L. *Calliandra grisebachii* (Br. & Rose) Standley (figure 10) *Diphysa carthagenensis* Jacq. (figure 21) *Salvia coccinea* L.
Painkillers	*Asclepias curassavica* L. (figure 4) *Guazuma ulmifolia* Lam. *Oxalis latifolia* Kunth *Plumeria* sp.
Rheumatism	*Asclepias curassavica* L. (figure 4) *Persea americana* Miller *Petiveria alliacea* L. *Zanthoxylum* sp.
Skin complaints *Metopium brownei* (Jacq.) Urban is a strong skin irritant that is also used to remove warts.	*Bursera simaruba* (L.) Sargent (figure 8) *Carica papaya* L. *Cassia villosa* Miller (figure 12) *Catasetum maculatum* Kunth (figure 13) *Citrus aurantifolia* L. *Citrus aurantium* (Christm.) Swingle *Croton* sp. *Euphorbia schlectendalii* Boiss. *Hamelia patens* Jacq. *Metopium brownei* (Jacq.) Urban *Ocimum micranthum* Willd. *Oxalis latifolia* Kunth *Persea americana* Miller *Psidium guajava* L. *Rhoeo discolor* (L'Her.) Hance *Rivina humilis* L. *Ruellia nudiflora* (Engelm. & Gray) Urban *Salvia coccinea* L. *Stigmaphyllon ellipticum* (Kunth) Juss.

TABLE 1 cont'd

Use	Plants
Soap	*Sapindus saponaria*
Stomach complaints	*Byrsonima crassifolia* (L.) Kunth (figure 9) *Callicarpa acuminata* Kunth *Citrus aurantium* (Christm.) Swingle *Cymbopogon citratus* Stapf. (figure 20) *Diphysa carthagenensis* Jacq. (figure 21) *Dorstenia contrajerva* L. *Jatropha gaumeri* Greenman (figure 25) *Ocimum micranthum* Willd. *Persea americana* Miller *Psidium guajava* L. *Ricinus communis* L. (figure 31) *Urera caracasana* (Jacq.) Griseb. (figure 36)
Winds, convulsions, epilepsy	*Bunchosia swartziana* Griseb. *Pedilanthus itzaeus* Millsp. *Zanthoxylum* sp.
Wounds, hemostats	*Bromelia pinguin* L. (figure 7) *Cydista potosina* (Schum. & Loes.) Loes. (figure 19) *Jatropha gaumeri* Greenman (figure 25)

CHAPTER SEVEN
Relation to Colonial Sources

Ralph Roys' (1931) study, *The Ethno-Botany of the Maya*, was the first in a new genre of works on the subject in that he transcribed, translated, and analyzed Maya texts and manuscripts from the colonial period (including the Mena and Sotuta manuscripts [Latin American Library at Tulane University, Mena Ms. and Sotuta Ms.], the Chilam Balam books of Nah, Ixil [Latin American Library at Tulane University, Ixil, Chilam Balam de. Ms.], and part of the Kaua [Latin American Library at Tulane University, Kaua, Chilam Balam de. Ms.]), instead of working solely from the Spanish texts. The latter class of documents was not, however, ignored. Roys also cataloged plants described in the Spanish manuscript, *Yerbas y hechicerías del Yucatán* (Latin American Library at Tulane University) (probably dating from the eighteenth century), which may have been the original of the "Book of the Jew" written by an Italian doctor named Ricardo Ossado, and an assortment of later works that may be seen as editions or derivatives of this most influential work. Roys prevailed upon his colleague, the famous botanist Paul Standley, to identify the plants he investigated in *The Ethno-Botany of the Maya*. Standley had completed *Trees and Shrubs of Mexico* between 1920 and 1926 and *Flora of Yucatan* in 1930. Both authors are recognized as pioneers in the fields of Yucatecan botany, ethnobotany, and ethnohistory sixty years later.

My collection of Yucatecan flora contained 178 numbers. Of these, 131 specimens have been identified at the species level (scientific binomial), 12 plants have been identified as far as their genus, and 14 have not been determined, adding up to a total of 157 plants. The remainder consists of duplicate specimens. Additionally, I collected information about two citrus species, for which I did not make voucher specimens. The following is an analysis of how my collection compares to the plants mentioned in *The Ethno-Botany of the Maya* (Roys 1931) and by extension, to the colonial sources studied by its author.

At the suggestion of my dissertation director, Dr. Victoria Bricker, I enlarged this comparison to include the plants mentioned in the second part of the *Book of Chilam Balam of Kaua*, the translation of which she generously made available to me for this purpose. Comparisons between my collection and the plants mentioned in the second part of the Kaua manuscript will be presented after comparisons to the plants of Roys' *Ethno-Botany*.

Comparisons with Roys' (1931) Ethno-Botany of the Maya

First, I compared the 131 plants in my collection that were identified most firmly (to the level of their species) to those mentioned in Roys' catalog. Ninety-eight species, or about 83 percent of that group of plants appeared there. Of the 98 plants, 55 (50 percent) were used by the modern-day curers I worked with in much the same way as their colonial-epoch antecedents. By this I mean that either the plant was specifically said to treat the same medical problem, was utilized in the same way (i.e., as a food resource or in the construction of an article of material culture), or that uses appeared to be strongly related; for example, one use I recorded for *Hamelia patens* is as a treatment for scrapes and welts. Among the uses recorded by Roys (1931:250) for the same plant is as a treatment for scrapes, "swellings of the legs," scabs, and snakebite. I conclude that the plant was and is employed in the treatment of a variety of skin ailments.

I am certain that the percentages of corresponding usages would be considerably higher if Roys had found a reference to the use of each plant mentioned in *Ethno-Botany of the Maya.* In eleven cases where the same binomial appears in my collection and Roys' *Ethno-Botany,* just a brief description of the plant's habit is noted, as provided by one or another of the botanists who established large collections in Yucatan, or Roys' translation of the common name recorded by the botanists appears. It seems likely that the medical manuscripts written in Maya and intended for a Maya audience might omit describing some of the most well-known or common plants, but would include ones that were exotic and therefore noteworthy to a Spaniard. In addition, I recorded numerous magical uses for plants, whereas the Spanish works analyzed by Roys are almost devoid of such references. Table 2 (starting on p. 80) contains the ninety-eight plants I collected that are mentioned in Roys (1931). A list of the fifty-five plants used today in at least one of the ways mentioned in Roys is found in appendix B.

In the interest of accuracy, I considered the twelve plants identified only to the level of genus to be part of the group of plants I labeled "Not mentioned in Roys." Examination of even this small subset of the data reinforced and reflected a concept that recurred throughout; namely, certain genera of plants were or are considered to be useful for treating certain "generic" types of medical problems. Seven of the twelve plants in this group were used in similar ways to other members of their genus (with no use having been recorded by Roys for the remaining five plants). This suggests that, for example, several *Gouania* species may be or may have been considered useful in the treatment of sores that appear in the mouths of patients and that several species of *Hyptis* are or were perceived as useful in treating stomach disorders. Table 3 (starting on p. 87) contains these correlations.

Another sizeable segment of the plants I grouped under the title "Not mentioned in Roys" may be categorized as being differing identifications for plants that bear the same or similar common names in both Roys' catalog and my own collection. These plants are presented in table 4 (starting on p. 89). There are sixteen such cases, with eight of this number belonging to the same genus. In other words, it is only rarely that the differing identifications of plants with the same common name apply to species belonging to different genera. This again supports the obvious conclusion that in both past and present times in Yucatan, the cognitive unit most important in the Maya system of plant knowledge is that of the folk genus. This is in accordance with the basic principles of ethnobotanical classification in traditional societies outlined by ethnobotanists Berlin, Breedlove, and Raven, who postulated as early as 1973 that generic taxa are the basic building blocks of folk taxonomy: genera are the most salient psychologically, and they are among the first taxa learned by children. When plants with the same common name do belong to different genera, in several cases the names could be considered descriptive terms providing information about either the use of the plant or its habit. For example, *Talinum triangulare* (figure 34) and *Pereskia aculeata* belong to different families (Portulacaceae and Cactaceae, respectively) but their common name, *dzum yahil*, means "shrinks swellings" and that is how both plants are utilized. *Calliandra grisebachii* (Leguminosae) (figure 10) and *Clematis dioica* (Ranunculaceae) share a common name, *mex nuxib*, which means "mustache," presumably because the leaves of both resemble a mustache.

Twenty-three plants in my collection appeared in Roys' *Ethno-Botany of the Maya* with the same scientific binomials, but very different common names. In six of the twenty-three cases, Roys' work gives Maya names for plants that I had recorded as having Spanish or Hispanicized names. In the remaining instances, a divergent Maya name was recorded for each plant. During my last trip to Yucatan, I succeeded in eliciting a Maya name from two curers for one of the plants for which they had previously given me only a Spanish name: *pata de vaca* (*Bauhinia divaricata* L., figure 5) was translated directly into the Maya and became *u y oc wacax* (not the *tsulub-tok* recorded by Roys). This small sample suggests that although some Maya plant names may have been replaced with Spanish names after circa 1930, the proportion of these plants is small compared to the majority of species examined here. On the whole, a comparison of my collection to the plants mentioned in Roys' *Ethno-Botany of the Maya* suggests a high degree of stability in both plant names and uses over a fairly long period of time.

The sources examined by Roys came from the same general region where I collected voucher specimens and recorded traditional Maya uses for them: northern Yucatan. It appears that the same set of plants has been considered either useful or medicinal at least since the colonial period and possibly before. I have already mentioned that the works studied by Roys may well have been compilations or editions of earlier, nonextant documents or manuscripts. The exact boundaries of this "region" remain to be tested, and it may well prove to extend across the rest of the peninsula to the south, east, and west of the area where I conducted this research. Dr. Victoria Bricker pointed out that many of the medical prescriptions found in the Chilam Balam books of Nah, Kaua, and Tekax (Latin American Library at Tulane University, Kaua, Chilam Balam de. Ms.; *Manuscritos de Tekax y Nah* 1981) are very similar, although the towns of provenience are located in different parts of the peninsula.

The curers with whom I worked are practicing in a relatively small part of Yucatan, but the majority of them moved there from elsewhere. The peninsula is still, as it has been at least since the colonial epoch, a place noted for extraordinary movement among its populace. Within the peninsula, there are no strong geographically bound divisions of land. The family of the father (and teacher) of one of the curers I have been working with near Chichén Itzá, for example, hails from Oxkutzcab in the southwest Puuc area. The plants he uses for practical and medicinal purposes are almost identical to those employed by other curers who originally came from towns to the southeast of Chichén Itzá. Despite the ebb and flow of the populations of Yucatan, those knowledgeable in the use of plants of both local and European origin seem to have relied upon the same set of plants for practical and medicinal problems for several centuries. Whether this knowledge will continue to be utilized remains to be seen. The younger generation is largely (and somewhat ironically) unaware of the movement in the United States and Europe toward natural remedies and products, and each curer has complained of the difficulty in locating certain plants that were previously common and easy to find.

It is not surprising to find that the largest categories of corresponding usages are those relating to the most common issues and problems of staying healthy in a tropical environment and contain the more common and well-known flora of the peninsula. The largest category of plants whose use appears to have remained stable over time is that of twenty-one species used to treat a variety of skin ailments and irritations, including rashes, sores, swellings, ringworm, and insect/snakebites. Any visitor to Yucatan will appreciate the necessity of having a wide range of accessible remedies available for these annoying problems.

Fifteen plants with edible fruit or seeds comprise the next largest category, followed by nine plants used to treat dysentery, diarrhea, and generalized stomach problems. There are many plants with more than one use; in particular, many of the well-known members of the former category serve "double duty" as medicinal resources, including *Annona squamosa, Bixa orellana, Brosimum alicastrum, Carica papaya, Citrus aurantium, Persea americana,* and *Psidium guajava.* The climate of Yucatan is warm all year round, with the incidence of amoebic dysentery, cholera, and the like increasing with the rainy season (Dr. Eduardo González Coeto, personal communication).

Smaller categories of use include five species used as painkillers, four used as diuretics, five remedies for fevers, five remedies for coughs, and two utilized in house construction. One plant was used specifically for earaches, another for eye complaints, and a third for convulsions or epilepsy. *Brosimum alicastrum* has apparently long been considered useful both as an edible plant and as a specific remedy for coughs, and the fruit of *Sapindus saponaria* is still employed, as in the past, as a soap. *Metopium brownei* is recognized as a strong skin irritant, to be avoided as in the past.

The following plants are the remaining binomials not mentioned in Roys (1931) and do not represent alternate identifications for plants with similar common names:

Cassia stenocarpa Vogel
Chlorophora tinctoria (L.) Gaud.
Croton miradorensis Muell. Arg.
Cymbopogon citratus Stapf. (figure 20)
Ficus radula Willd.
Hymenocallis americana Roem.
Melochia pyramidata L.
Phaseolus atropurpureus DC.
Plumeria obtusa L.
Salvia micrantha Vahl
Solanum nudum Kunth
Solanum tequilense Gray
Spilanthes filipes Greenm.
Stigmaphyllon ellipticum (Kunth) Juss.
Talinum paniculatum (Jacq.) Gaertn. (figure 33)

Comparison with the Second Volume of the Kaua Manuscript

A slightly different methodology was employed for comparing my plant collection to the plants mentioned in the Kaua manuscript, since the only reliable variables available in that work are the Maya common name and the use(s) described for the plant that bears it. A search for plants with similar common names in both my collection and Dr. Victoria Bricker's translation of the second volume of the Kaua manuscript yielded sixty "matches." Included are "matches" between binomials and plants identified only to genera. Of the sixty "matches," slightly more than 50 percent (thirty-two plants) were used in similar ways. Table 5 (starting on p. 91) contains a comparison of the common names and similar uses of the thirty-two plants in the latter group. In the interest of uniformity within this text and ease of use, plants are presented in the alphabetic order of the scientific names in my collection. Table 6 (starting on p. 94) is similarly ordered and contains the sixty common names found in both works.

The three largest categories of use were skin complaints, stomach problems, and edible plants, as they were in my previous comparison to the plants mentioned by Roys. Thirteen plants were employed for treating skin ailments. This was the largest category of use. Plants used to treat stomach complaints (ten plants) comprised the next largest category. The remaining plants were utilized as painkillers, treatments for diseases of the eyes, and fever reducers and included one hemostat and one treatment for evil eye. Only four edible plants were mentioned: papaya, guava, a chile pepper, and an orange. Of these, only the chile and the papaya were specifically said to be edible plants. The intended audience of the Kaua manuscript would have been literate Mayas, who were no doubt already familiar with these resources.

The plant names in the second volume of the Kaua manuscript are very close or identical to those I recorded. That they would be even closer than those appearing in Roys' *The Ethno-Botany of the Maya* is not surprising, because the town of Kaua itself is located a short distance from where I collected voucher specimens and recorded common names. All the plants mentioned in the second volume of the Kaua manuscript also appear in Roys' (1931) *The Ethno-Botany of The Maya.*

TABLE 2

Comparison of Common Names and Uses of Plants with Similar
Scientific Binomials in Both My Collection and Roys' *Ethno-Botany* (1931)

The first column lists the scientific binomial for each of the ninety-eight plants in this
group. If a modern version of a scientific name exists, it will be listed first, with the
synonym from Roys (1931) following in parentheses. The second column contains the
applicable Maya and Spanish common names from Roys (R) and my collection (K).
The third column lists any corresponding uses between the data in my collection and
Roys' *Ethno-Botany*; if the uses are different, a "D" will appear; if no use was mentioned by Roys an "O" will appear.

Scientific Binomial	Comparison of Common Names	Comparison of Uses
Abrus precatorius L. (figure 1)	R. xoco-ak K. oxoh, coral negro del monte	D
Ageratum conyzoides L. (*Ageratum gaumeri* Millsp.)	R. zac-mizib K. x holon al (sac misib = *Abutilon permolle* (Willd.) Sweet in my collection)	D
Annona glabra L.	R. h-maak K. op, annona	Edible fruit
Annona squamosa L.	R. tsalmuy K. saramuyo (Hispanicization of Maya name)	Edible fruit. Fever, chills, head cold *(catarro)*
Apoplanesia paniculata Presl. (figure 3)	R. chulul K. kik che	D
Asclepias curassavica L. (figure 4)	R. anal-kak, anal-xiu K. x anal	Painkiller
Astrocasia phyllanthoides Rob. & Millsp.	R. kah-yuc, ppix-thon-kax K. x kah yuc	O
Bauhinia divaricata L. (figure 5)	R. tsulub tok K. pata de vaca, u y oc wacax	R. Pleurisy K. Coughing with blood
Bixa orellana L.	R. kuxub K. kiwi, achiote	Condiment, coloring agent, treatment of red eruptions with red seeds? R. Erysipelas, cimex eruptions (smallpox) K. Measles
Blechum pyramidatum (Juss.) Urban (figure 6)	R. akab-xiu K. x akab xiu, x aka xiu	Fevers

TABLE 2 cont'd

Scientific Binomial	Comparison of Common Names	Comparison of Uses
Borreria laevis (Lam. Griseb. (*Spermacoce tenuior* L.) (*Spermacoce verticillata* L.)	R. x-ta-ulmil, ni-zotz (respectively) K. menta kax	O
Borreria pulchra Millsp.	R. bacal-che, kakal-che K. bacal che, baca che	D
Bromelia pinguin L. (figure 7)	R. piñuela, tzalbay K. piñuela, ch'om	D
Brosimum alicastrum Swartz.	R. ox, ramón K. ox, ramón	Edible fruit R. Phthisis K. Coughs
Bunchosia swartziana Griseb. (*Bunchosia glandulosa* Cav. DC.)	R. zip-ché K. sip che	Convulsions, epilepsy (caused by evil winds)
Bursera simaruba (L.) Sarg. (figure 8) *Byrsonima crassifolia* (L.) Kunth (figure 9)	R. chacah K. chacah R. zac pah, nancen agria K. nance, chi	Skin ailments, snakebite, fever Edible fruit
Caesalpinia gaumeri Greenm.	R. citam-che, citin-che K. citan che	D
Calea urticifolia L.	R. xicin K. x kah xicin	Skin ailments
Callicarpa acuminata Kunth	R. zac-puc-yim K. x pukim	O
Capsicum annuum L.	R. ic, max-ic K. chile max, max ic	Edible fruit
Carica papaya L.	R. put, chich-put K. ch'ich' put	Edible fruit, skin ailments
Casimiroa tetrameria Millsp.	R. yuy, h-yuy K. yuy	R. Leaves used for "diarrhea accompanied by chills" K. Leaves used for fever
Cassia atomaria L. (*Cassia emarginata* L.)	R. x-tu-ab, x-tu-habin K. x tu habin, x tu habim	D
Cassia villosa Miller (figure 12)	R. zal-che K. sal che	Skin ailments
Catasetum maculatum Kunth (figure 13)	R. chit-kuk, chit-cuuc K. ch'it cuc	Sores, abscesses

TABLE 2 cont'd

Scientific Binomial	Comparison of Common Names	Comparison of Uses
Cecropia peltata L. (*Cecropia obtusa* Trecul)	R. x-coch-le K. koch	Diuretic qualities employed. R. Retention of urine K. Diabetes
Cedrela mexicana M. Roem.	R. kuche, kulche K. cedro	Wood used in construction, earache
Ceiba aesculifolia 　(Kunth) Britt. & Baker 　(figures 14 and 15)	R. pochote, choo K. yax che, pochote, ceiba	D
Cissus rhombifolia Vahl	R. tab-can, x-tab-canil K. x tab canil, x ta canih	D
Cissus sicyoides L.	R. yax-tab-canil K. x tab canil, x ta canih	D
Citrus aurantium 　(Christm.) Swingle (*Citrus amara* Link)	R. chuhuc-pakal 　(a mistake? ch'uhuc 　= sweet, and *Citrus* 　*sinensis* L. is sweet orange) K. naranjo agrío, pakal	R. Buboes K. Bruises, *bilis*
Cnidoscolus chayamansa 　McVaugh (figure 16), *Cnidoscolus aconitifolius* 　(Mill.) I. M. Johnston 　—of Roys p.p. (*Jatropha aconitifolia* Mill.) (*Jatropha urens* L.) 　Edible species in the 　group were divided by 　McVaugh post-Roys	R. chay, chaya, chinchin-chay, tzintzin-chay, x-tzah for *J. aconitifolia* chinchin-chay, tzintzin-chay for *J. urens.* K. chay, chaya	Edible leaves, purgative qualities
Coccoloba uvifera L.	R. nii-che, uva del mar K. uva del mar	Edible fruit
Colubrina greggii S. Watson	R. puc-yim, pucim K. balsamo de los Mayas	Pain killer
Cordia dodecandra A.DC.	R. kop-té, siricote K. kop te, siricote	Edible fruit
Crataeva tapia L. (figure 18)	R. kolok-max, tres marías K. tres marías	D
Croton cortesianus Kunth	R. sac-xiu K. sac xiu	D
Croton flavens L.	R. xabalam K. xicin burro, xicim burro, orejón del burro	R. Snakebite, "chills accompanied by diarrhea" K. Sores in the mouth

TABLE 2 cont'd

Scientific Binomial	Comparison of Common Names	Comparison of Uses
Croton humilis L.	R. ic-aban R. sores, ulcers K. x ic aban, hic aban	R. sores, ulcers K. warts
Cyperus ochraceus Vahl	R. mazcab-zuuc, x-chab-xan, x-cabal-xaan K. x cambal xan, x camba xan	D
Diphysa carthagenensis Jacq. (figure 21)	R. tsutsuc, x-tsutsuc K. dzudzuc	Dysentery
Dorstenia contrajerva L.	R. x-cambal-hau K. cambal hau, camba hau	Stomach problems, including dysentery and colic
Ehretia tinifolia L. (figure 22)	R. beec K. bec	D
Elytraria imbricata (Vahl) Pers. (*Elytraria squamosa* (Jacq.) Lindau)	R. x-cabal-xaan K. cambal xan, camba xan	D
Erythrina standleyana Krukoff (*Erythrina americana* Mill.) (*Erythrina coralloides* Mocq. & Sesse)	R. chac-mol-che, colorin K. chac mol che	Eye complaints
Eupatorium odoratum L. (figure 23) (*Eupatorium conyzoides* Mill.) (*Trixis radialis* [L.] Kuntze.)	R. tok-aban K. x tok aban, x tok abam	R. Blood in the urine, malaria, gonorrhea K. Retention of urine
Euphorbia schlectendalii Boiss.	R. zac-chacah K. sac chacah	Skin ailments
Evolvulus alsiniodes Boiss.	R. yax-xiu, x-yax-xiu K. x puluc xom (Dr. V. Bricker suggests this may be a corruption of x purgación)	O
Gossypium hirsutum L.	R. taman, algodón atabacado K. taman, tamam	R. Asthma K. Coughs
Guazuma ulmifolia Lam.	R. pixoy K. pixoy	R. Cramps, abdominal pains K. Labor pains
Hamelia patens Jacq.	R. x-kanan K. x kanan	Skin ailments

TABLE 2 cont'd

Scientific Binomial	Comparison of Common Names	Comparison of Uses
Helicteres barvensis Jacq.	R. zutup, tzutup K. suput, sutup	D
Hibiscus poeppigii (Sprengel) Garcke (*Hibiscus tubiflorus* DC.)	R. x-tup-kinil, tupkin K. x tup kinil	Swellings, inflammations
Indigofera suffruticosa Mill. (*Indigofera anil* L.)	R. ch'oh K. ch'oh	D
Ipomoea tiliaceae (Willd.) Choisy (*Ipomoea fastigiata* Sweet)	R. hebil K. yax ceiyli	O
Jatropha curcas L. (figure 24)	R. x-cacal-che, zicilté, avellanas K. ponpon che, ponpoche	O
Jatropha gaumeri Greenman (figure 25)	R. x-pomol che K. pomol che	Dysentery, purgative
Kallstroemia maxima (L.) Torr. & Gray (*Tribulus maximus* L.)	R. xichil-ak K. chitun kax	O
Lepidium virginicum L.	R. x-put-can, mastuerzo K. altanisa	D
Leucaena leucocephala (Lam.) de Witt (*Leucocephala glauca* [L.] Benth.)	R. uaxim K. uaxim	Different uses, but both note that eating the plant causes animals' tails to fall out. Roys does not mention that seeds are edible; perhaps because practice was introduced by people from central Mexico?
Lonchocarpus longistylus Pittier (figure 26)	R. balche K. balche	Ceremonial wine
Malmea depressa (Baillon) Fries (*Guatteria gaumeri* Greenman)	R. ele-muy, conejo quemado K. elemuyil	D
Merremia dissecta (Jacq.) Hallier F. (*Ipomoea sinuata* Ortega)	R. hunab-tzotz K. ha'as ak	Roys states that the plant is a cure for seven unidentified diseases named for seven planets
Metopium brownei (Jacq.) Urban	R. chechem, grenadillo K. chechem	Skin irritant

TABLE 2 cont'd

Scientific Binomial	Comparison of Common Names	Comparison of Uses
Mimosa pudica L.	R. x-mutz K. x mudz	D
Momordica charantia L.	R. cundeamor, yacunah-ak K. chincha mora, cundeamor	Edible
Morinda yucatanensis Greenman	R. x-hoyoc, x-hoyen-cab K. piña de culebra	D
Nopalea inaperta Schott ex Griffin	R. tzacam-zotz K. x pakam	O
Ocimum micranthum Willd.	R. x-cacal-tun, albahaca K. x cacal tun	R. Buboes, "Blood in the feces," dysentery K. Pimples, dysentery
Oxalis latifolia Kunth	R. yala-elel K. yala elel, yala eleh	Skin ailments, swellings
Parthenium hysterophorus L.	R. hauay K. pulmonia xiu	D
Passiflora foetida L.	R. tuu-boc, x-tu-can K. poch, (x-boc?)	Poulticed on sores
Pedilanthus itzaeus Millsp.	R. yax-halalche K. yax halal che	D
Persea americana Miller (*Persea gratissima* Gaertn.)	R. on, aguacate K. on, aguacate	Edible fruit, diarrhea, skin treatment
Petiveria alliacea L.	R. pay-che, zorrillo K. pay che	D
Phaseolus elegans Piper	R. kanalzin K. x cap xiu	D
Piper auritum Kunth (figure 28)	R. xmakulam K. maculan, maculam, yerba santa	D
Piscidia piscipula L. Sargent (figure 29) (*Piscidia erythrina* L.) (*Ichthyomethia communis* Blake)	R. habin K. habin, habim	House construction R. Asthma K. Coughs
Plantago major L. (figure 30)	R. yanten, llanten K. llanten	D
Porophyllum punctatum (Miller) Blake	R. x-pech-ukil, uk-che K. x pech' ukil	D

TABLE 2 cont'd

Scientific Binomial	Comparison of Common Names	Comparison of Uses
Portulaca oleracea L.	R. verdolaga, cabal-chum, xucul K. verdolaga	D Again, Roys does not mention that leaves are edible: a recent European innovation?
Priva lappulacea (L.) Pers.	R. tzayuntzay K. x opol	O
Psidium guajava L.	R. pichi, guayabo K. pichi, guayaba	Edible fruit, diarrhea
Psittacanthus americanus (Jacq.) Mart.	R. keb, x-keu K. kubem ba	Skin irritations, buboes
Rauwolfia heterophylla L.	R. cabal-muc K. cabal muc, caba muc	Sores
Rhoeo discolor (L'Her.) Hance	R. chac-tsam K. morado che, chac tzab	Skin treatment
Ricinus communis L.	R. x-kach, higuerilla K. sac koch, koch blanco	R. "Pain in the bowels" K. Worms, laxative
Rivina humilis L.	R. kuxub-can K. sabac pox	Skin irritations
Salvia coccinea L.	R. chac-tzitz K. chac lol, chac tzits	R. Cavities in teeth K. Sores
Sapindus saponaria L.	R. zihom, zihum K. jaboncillo	Soap
Selenicereus donkelaarii (Salm.-Dyck)	R. tzacam-ak, zac-bacel-can K. tzacam ak, kan choch	Skin ailments
Sida acuta Burm. (figure 32)	R. chichibé K. chichi be	Coughs, asthma
Tagetes erecta L. (*Tagetes patula* L.)	R. x-puhuk, maceual puhuk, pastora K. x tempula xiu, tempula	O
Tecoma stans (L.) Kunth	R. x-kan-lol, tronadores K. kan lol	D
Thevetia gaumeri Helmsl.	R. acitz, campanilla, cabalonga K. pisté	O
Thouinia paucidentata Radlk. (figure 35)	R. kan-chunup K. x kan chunup	O
Urera caracasana (Jacq.) Griseb. (figure 36)	R. laal, la, ortiga	Stomach complaints
(*Urera microcarpa* Wedd.)	K. lal, ortiga K. Body aches	R. Aching bones

TABLE 3

Twelve Plants Identified to Genus Only in My Collection,
Compared with Similar Species in Roys (1931)

The first column lists plants identified to genera only, with the common name(s) I collected for them. The second column shows the "best matches" found in Roys (1931) in terms of species or common name. If a modern version of the scientific name exists, it will be listed first, with the synonym from Roys following in parentheses. The third column provides a comparison of the uses noted in the *Ethno-Botany* (R) to those I collected (K).

Genus/Common Name in My Collection	Species within Genus and Common Name in Roys (1931)	Comparison of uses
Anthurium sp. x buc tum	*Anthurium tetragonum* Engl. box kutz	R. no use given K. purgative
Catasetum sp. ch'it cuc	*Catasetum maculatum* Kunth (figure 13) chit-kuk	R. poulticed on sores K. same use
Cordia sp. kop te	*Cordia dodecandra* A.DC. kopté, chac-kopté	R. no use given K. fruit is edible, leaves are used to scrub pots
Cyperus sp. x cambal xan, x camba xan	*Cyperus ochraceus* Vahl mazcab-zuuc *Cyperus uncinatus* Poir. x-cabal-xan	R. no use given K. combined with *Dorstenia contrajerva* L. to treat infertility
Ficus cotinifolia Kunth akum *Ficus* sp. as copo, alamo	*Ficus cotinifolia* Kunth x-copó and *Ficus mexicanus* Miq. as zac-cab-ha	R. the former is used for "abscess of the ear." No use for the latter. K. used to heal umbilical cord
Gouania sp. om xiu	*Gouania lupuloides* (L.) Urban (*Gouania dominguensis* L.) om-ak	R. sores in the mouth, "blood vomit," and "rotten liver" K. Mouth sores and pimples
Hyptis sp. and *H. suaveolens*	*Hyptis pectinata* (L.) Poit. chac sikin xolté-x-nuc	R. dysentery, "night fevers" (L.)Poit. K. stomach pains, vomiting
Passiflora sp. x po kinil	Several *Passiflora* species are listed, none with similar common names. *P. foetida* L. has a similar use.	R. *P. foetida* L. used for swellings, sores, and ringworm. K. *P. foetida* L. is edible, while the *Passiflora* sp. is used on venereal sores.

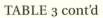

TABLE 3 cont'd

Genus/Common Name in My Collection	Species within Genus and Common Name in Roys (1931)	Comparison of uses
Phyllanthus sp. cancer kax	Three *Phyllanthus* species, all with different names. *P. conami* Swartz. has a similar use, and *P. nobilis* (L.) Muell. is described as "ointment tree"	R. *P. conami* Swartz used for buboes and skin eruptions. K. applied to "external cancers."
Piper sp. yax pelech ché	*Piper gaumeri* Trel. (*Piper medium* Jacq.) yax-ppehel-che, x-pehel-che	R. headaches K. headaches
Spermacoce sp. buy	*Spermacoce verticillata* L. and *S. tenuior* Lam. ni-tzotz and x-ta-ulmil, respectively	R. no use given for either *Spermacoce* sp. K. "fleshy growths in the eyes" *(carnosidad)*
Zanthoxylum sp. tamcaz che, x tancaz che	*Zanthoxylum fagara* (L.) Sarg. tamcaz-che, tancaz-che. *Z. caribaeum* Lam. zinan-che	R. the former *Zanthoxylum* "cures every disease." The latter is used for headache, dysentery. K. headaches and other body aches, including rheumatism. Also, as a protective amulet.

TABLE 4

Plants with the Same or Similar Common Name as in Roys (1931),
but with Differing Identifications

The first column contains the binomial and common names as they appear in my collection, the second column lists the same information as it appears in Roys' *Ethno-Botany of the Maya*, and the third column provides a comparison of uses for each species. If no use appears in Roys (1931), an "O" will appear; if they are different, a "D" will appear. Complete information on uses may be found in appendix A.

Common Name and Scientific Binomial—Kunow collection	Common Name and Scientific Binomial—Roys	Comparison of Uses
sac misib *Abutilon permolle* (Willd.) Sweet	zac-mizbil *Abutilon trisulcatum* (Jacq.) Urban zac-mizib *Ageratum gaumeri* Millsp., *Waltheria americana* L.	Skin complaints (second sp. Roys)
subin, subim *Acacia collinsii* Safford (figure 2) All *Acacia* species mentioned are ant acacias	zubin, zubin-che, cornezuelo *Acacia cornigera* (L.) Willd. (*Acacia globulifera* Safford) *Platymiscium yucatanensis* Standl.	D
sac pah *Byrsonima bucidaefolia* Standley	zac-pah *Byrsonima crassifolia* (L.) Kunth (figure 9)	Edible fruit
x mex nuxib, x mex nuxih *Calliandra grisebachii* (Br. & Rose) Standley (figure 10)	mex-nuxib *Clematis dioica* L.	D
xek ixil, xek ixih *Cydista potosina* Loes. (Schum. & Loes.) (figure 19)	x-ek-kixil, ek-kixil-ak *Bignonia unguis-cati* L.	D
chac motz *Dalea nutans* (Cav.) Willd.	chac motz *Sicydium tamnifolium* Jacq.	O
xanab mucuy, xana mucuy *Euphorbia hypericifolia* L.	yerba del pollo, xanab-mucuy for *Euphorbia hirta* L. (notes that the latter common name is applied to several of *Euphorbia* species)	R. Strangury K. Retention of urine

TABLE 4 cont'd

Common Name and Scientific Binomial—Kunow collection	Common Name and Scientific Binomial—Roys	Comparison of Uses
hol, agujero *Hampea integerrima* Schlechtendal	hol *Hibiscus tubiflorus* DC. x-holol *Hibiscus elatus* Swartz	D
xic tzotz *Passiflora pulchella* Kunth	xik-tzotz *Passiflora coriacea* Juss.	D The common name, "bat's wing," seems to be generally descriptive of the shape of the leaves of several *Passifloras*
x maculan silvestre, x makulam silvestre *Piper amalago* L.	maculan, ix-maculan *Piper auritum* Kunth (figure 28)	D *P. amalago* is the "wild" *Piper*
x cabal yaxnic, x camba yax nic *Ruellia nudiflora* (Engelm. & Gray) Urban	x-cabal-yaxnic, yerba de la calentura, maravilla del monte *Ruellia tuberosa* L.	R. Swollen breasts, "sore mouth" K. Kidney inflammation
yerba mora *Solanum americanum* Miller	yerba mora, pahal-can *Solanum nigrum* L.	R. Skin ailments, swellings, snakebite K. Burns
buy *Spermacoce tetraquetra* A. Rich	buy, buy-ak *Serjania adiantoides* Radlk.	Eye complaints
dzum yahil, dzum yahih' *Talinum triangulare* (Jacq.) Willd. (figure 34)	dzum-ya, dzum-yail *Pereskia aculeata* Mill.	Swellings The common name means "shrinks swellings"
x akab xiu, sac sahun *Tridax procumbens* L.	akab-xiu *Blechum pyramidatum* (Juss.) Urban (figure 6)	D This may have been a misidentification on the part of the curer, with whom I also collected *B. pyramidatum* as x akab xiu

ixim che
Urechites andrieuxii
    Muell. Arg
	ixim-che
	Casearia nitida
	    (L.) Jacq.,
	Citharexylum schottii
	    Greenm.,
	Andira inermis Kunth
		Cramps

TABLE 5

Comparison of Thirty-two Plants with Similar Common Names and Uses in My Collection and the Second Volume of the Kaua Manuscript

The first column lists the scientific name for a plant in my collection. Divergent identifications from Dr. V. Bricker's translation follow. The second column lists the common name as it appears in the Kaua manuscript, and the third column lists the common name as I recorded it. The last column lists similar uses, with those from the Kaua manuscript listed first if they were not identical.

Scientific name	Kaua name	Kunow name	Similar uses
Asclepias curassavica L. (figure 4)	anal kak, cochinita	x anal	1) Swollen breast 2) Swollen gums, toothache
K. *Blechum pyramidatum* (Juss.) Urban (figure 6) B.(*Blechum pyramidatum* [Lam.] Urban)	akab xiu	x akab xiu, x aka xiu	"Night sweats" and "night fever"
K. *Bunchosia swartziana* Griseb.B. (*Bunchosia glandulosa* [Cav.] DC.)	sip che	sip che	1) "Aire" 2) Vientos malos
Bursera simaruba Sargent (figure 8)	chacah	chacah	Fever and skin (L.) complaints
Callicarpa acuminata Kunth	puc yim	x pukim	Vomiting and dysentery
Capsicum annuum L.	yc, max yc	max ik, chile max	Stomach complaints and edible
Carica papaya L.	put	ch'ich' put	Skin ailments and edible
Catasetum maculatum Kunth (figure 13)	ch'it cuc	ch'it cuc	1) Swellings and abscesses 2) Sores
Ceiba aesculifolia (Kunth) Britt. & Baker (figures 14 and 15)	pochote	pochote, yax che, ceiba	1) Swellings 2) Boys are said to grow breasts if they play with fruit

TABLE 5 cont'd

Scientific name	Kaua name	Kunow name	Similar uses
K. *Citrus aurantium* (Christm.) Swingle B. *Citrus sinensis* Osbeck	pakal	pakal, naranjo agrío pakal is a generic name for different species of oranges	1) Buboes, "heartpain" 2) Bruises, *bilis*
Croton humilis L.	ic haban	x ic aban, hic aban	1) Scrofula 2) Warts
Diphysa carthagenensis Jacq. (figure 21)	ix dzudzuc	dzudzuc	Purulent dysentery and 1) eruptions of the eye 2) *ojo*
Dorstenia contrajerva L.	x canbal hau	cambal hau, camba hau	Stomach complaints
K. *Erythrina standleyana* Krukoff B. (*Erythrina americana* Mill.)	chac mol che	chac mol che	Eye complaints
K. *Eupatorium odoratum* L. (figure 23) B. *Trixis inula* Crantz	tok aban	x tok aban, x tok abam	1) Retention of urine 2) To pass stones
K. *Euphorbia hypericifolia* L. B. *Euphorbia hirta* L.	xanab mucuy	xanab mucuy, xana mucuy, zapatos de tortolas	1) Retention of urine 2) To pass stones
K. *Gouania* sp. B. *Gouania lupuloides* (L.) Urban	x om ak	om xiu	Rashes and pimples
Guazuma ulmifolia Lam.	pixoy	pixoy	1) Cramping diarrhea 2) Lessens labor pains and hastens delivery
Hamelia patens Jacq.	x kanan	x kanan	Skin complaints
Jatropha guameri Greenman	pomol che	pomol che	To staunch hemorrhages
Ocimun micranthum Willd.	ix cacal tun	x cacal tun,	Dysentery
K. *Oxalis latifolia* Kunth	yala elel, matzab kuch, ch'oh chakan	yalah eleh	Skin complaints
B. *Oxalis yucatanensis* (Rose) Riley			Pain killer

TABLE 5 cont'd

Scientific name	Kaua name	Kunow name	Similar uses
K. *Plumeria obtusa* L. B. *Plumeria*	nicte	nicte ch'om nicte is a generic name for several Plumerias	Pain killer
Psidium guajava L.	chac pichi	pichi	Dysentery, diarrhea
RauwolWa heterophylla	cabal muc, cha muc	cabal muc, caba muc	1) Mange 2) Sores
Ricinus communis L. (figure 31)	koch, xochil	sac koch, koch blanco	1) Dysentery 2) Fever
K. *Ruellia nudiXora* Engelm. & Gray Urban B. *Ruellia tuberosa* L.	cabal yax nic, che ah suc, maravilla, pix lumil	x cabal yax nic, x camba yax nic	Swellings
K. *Selenicereus donkelaarii* B. (*Cereus donkelaarii* Salm Dyck	cantzacam sac bacel can	tzacam ak, kan choch	1) Snakebite 2) Bucal rashes
K. *Spermacoce tetraquetra* A. Rich B. *Serjania goniovarpa* Radlk.	buy ak	buy	Cataracts
K. *Talinum triangulare* (Jacq.) Willd. (figure 34) B. *Talinum paniculatum* (Jacq.) Gaertn. (figure 33)	dzum ya	dzum yahil, dzum yahih' The name, "shrinks swellings" is applied to various plants similarly used	Swellings
K. *Urera caracasana* (Jacq.) Griseb. (figure 36) B. *Urera* sp.	lal	lal, ortiga	1) Blood vomit 2) Stomach/ bladder pains
B. *Zanthoxylum fagara* (L.) Sarg.	x tancaz che		2) Evil winds (cause convulsions)

TABLE 6

All Similar Common Names of Plants in Both the Second Volume
of the Kaua Manuscript and in My Collection

The first column contains the scientific name for the plant in my collection.
Any divergent identifications for the Kaua common name from Dr. V. R.
Bricker's translation follow. The second column contains the common name
as it appears in the second volume of the Kaua manuscript, and the last column contains the common name as I recorded it.

Scientific name(s)	Common name—Kaua	Common name—Kunow
Annona squamosa L.	op	op
Asclepias curassavica L. (figure 4)	anal kak, cochinita	x anal
Astrocasia phyllanthoides Rob. & Millsp.	kah yuc	x kah yuc
Blechum pyramidatum (Juss.) Urban (figure 6)	akab xiu	x akab xiu, x aka xiu
Borreria pulchra Millsp.	bacal che	bacal che, baca che
K. *Bromelia pinguin* L. (figure 7) B. *Bromelia karatus* L.	chac ch'om	ch'om, piñuela
Brosimum alicastrum Sw.	ox	ox
K. *Bunchosia swartziana* Griseb. B. (*Bunchosia glandulosa* [Cav.] DC.)	sip che	sip che
Bursera simaruba (L.) Sarg. (figure 8)	chacah	chacah
K. *Byrsonima crassifolia* (L.) Kunth (figure 9) B. *Malphigia glabra* L.	chi	chi, nance
Callicarpa acuminata HBK	puc yim	x pukim
Capsicum annuum L.	yc, max yc	max ik, chile max
Carica papaya L.	put	ch'ich' put
K. *Cassia villosa* Miller (figure 12) B. *Cassia* sp.	sal che	sal che

TABLE 6 cont'd

Scientific name(s)	Common name—Kaua	Common name—Kunow
Catasetum maculatum Kunth (figure 13)	ch'it cuc	ch'it cuc
Ceiba aesculifolia (Britt. & Baker K. (figures 14 and 15)	pochote	pochote, yax che, ceiba
Cissus rhombifolia Vahl. B. *Cissus sicyoides* L.	tab can, x ta canil (For *Cissus sicyoides*)	x tab canil, x ta canih (For both species)
K. *Citrus aurantifolia* (Christm.) Swingle B. *Citrus sinensis* Osbeck	pakal	pakal, naranjo agrío
Cnidoscolus chayamansa McVaugh (figure 16)	chay	chay, chaya
Croton humilis L.	ic haban	x ic aban, hic aban
Diphysa carthagenensis Jacq. (figure 21)	ix dzudzuc	dzudzuc
Dorstenia contrajerva L.	x canbal hau	cambal hau, camba hau
Ehretia tinifolia L. (figure 22)	bec	bec
Elytraria imbricata (Vahl) Pers.	cabal xan	cambal xan, camba xan
K. *Erythrina standleyana* Krukoff B. (*Erythrina americana* Mill.)	chac mol che	chac mol che
K. *Eupatorium odoratum* L. (figure 23) B. *Trixis inula* Crantz	tok aban	x tok aban, x tok abam
K. *Euphorbia hypericifolia* L. B. *Euphorbia hirta* L.	xanab mucuy	xanab mucuy, xana' mucuy
K. *Ficus* sp. B. *Ficus cotinifolia* Kunth	copo	copo, alamo
Gossypium hirsutum L.	taman	taman, tamam
K. *Gouania* sp. B. *Gouania lupuloides* (L.) Urb.	x om ak	om xiu
Guazuma ulmifolia Lam.	pixoy	pixoy
Hamelia patens Jacq.	x kanan	x kanan

TABLE 6 cont'd

Scientific name(s)	Common name—Kaua	Common name—Kunow
Helicteres barvensis Jacq.	sutup	suput, sutup
K. *Hibiscus poeppigii* (Spreng.) Garcke	tup kin	x tup kinil
B. *Kosteletzkya tubiflora* (DC.) Blanchard & McVaugh		
K. *Hymenocallis americana* Roem. B. *Hymenocallis americana* [Jacq.] Salisb.	lirio	lirio blanco
Indigofera suffruticosa Miller	ch'oh	ch'oh
Jatropha gaumeri Greenman (figure 25)	pomol che	pomol che
Leucaena leucocephala (Lam.) de Witt	uaxim	uaxim
Metopium brownei (Jacq.) Urban	chechem	chechem
Ocimum micranthum Willd.	ix cacal tun	x cacal tun, albahaca
K. *Oxalis latifolia* Kunth B. *Oxalis yucatanensis* (Rose) Riley	yala elel, ch'oh chakan, matzab kuch	yala elel, yala eleh
K. *Pedilanthus itzaeus* Millsp. B. *Pedilanthus* sp.	yaax halal che	yax halal che
Petiveria alliacea L.	pay che	pay che
Piper auritum Kunth (figure 28)	makulan	makulan, makulam, yerba santa
Piscidia piscipula (L.) Sarg. (figure 29)	habin	habin, habim
Plantago major L. (figure 30)	llantén	llanten
K. *Plumeria obtusa* L. B. *Plumeria* sp.	nicte	nicte ch'om
Porophyllum punctatum (Miller) Blake	x pech' ukil, uk che	x pech' ukil
Psidium guajava L.	chac pichi	pichi

TABLE 6 cont'd

Scientific name(s)	Common name—Kaua	Common name—Kunow
K. *Rauwolfia heterophylla* L. B. (*Rauwolfia heterophylla* R. & S.)	chac muc, cabal muc	cabal muc, caba muc
K. *Ricinus communis* L. (figure 31) B. *Cecropia peltata* L. in my collection shares this common name	koch, xochil	sac koch, koch blanco for *R. communis* koch, guarumbo for *C. peltata*
K. *Ruellia nudiflora* (Engelm. & Gray) Urban B. *Ruellia tuberosa* L.	cabal yax nic, che ah suc	x cabal yax nic, x camba yax nic
K. *Selenicereus donkelaarii* (Salm.-Dyck) Br. & Rose B. (*Cereus donkelaarii* Salm.-Dyck)	can tzacam, sac bacel can	tzacam ak, kan choch
K. *Sida acuta* Burm. (figure 31) B. *Melochia tomentosa* L.	sac chichi be	chichi be
K. *Spermacoce tetraquetra* A. Rich B. *Serjania goniocarpa* Radlk.	buy	buy
Talinum paniculatum (Jacq.) Gaertn. (figure 33) and *Talinum triangulare* (Jacq.) Willd. (figure 34) share this common name in my collection. The former is the identification for the *Kaua* plant	dzum ya	dzum yahil, dzum yahih
Tecoma stans (L.) Kunth	kan lol	kan lol
Thouinia paucidentata Radlk. (figure 35)	kan chunup	x kan chunup
K. *Urera caracasana* (Jacq.) Griseb. (figure 36) B. *Urera* sp.	lal	lal, ortiga
K. *Zanthoxylum* sp. B. *Zanthoxylum fagara* (L.) Sarg.	tamcaz che	tamcaz che, x tancaz che

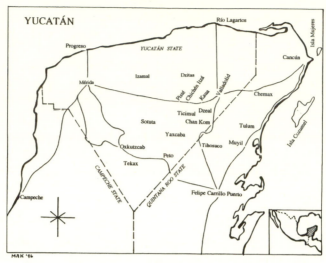

Map 1. Northern Yucatan (by Marianna Appel Kunow).

CHAPTER EIGHT

Conclusion

The curers with whom I worked in Yucatan share a tradition of plant use and ethnomedicine. There is a fairly large set of plants that is considered to be useful or medicinal among curers in the northern part of the peninsula. I suspect that the plants in this collection are but a fragment of that set, because I have not yet been able to conduct field research and collect plants during each month of the year. Although the curers may use these plants differently than their colleagues, the same plant names are mentioned again and again. When the common names are applied to different species, they often belong to the same genus. Some Yucatecan plant names appear to be descriptive of the medicinal or physical qualities of the plants. Interestingly, a similar system of classification is present in the Badianus manuscript, from the early colonial period near Mexico City (see Emmart 1940 and Guerra 1952).

The same set of plants has been used by curers for at least several hundred years, often in similar ways. The colonial sources to which I compared my collection may well be compilations of still earlier works, so that the temporal boundaries of this regional oral tradition are difficult to determine. The curers of Yucatan are heirs to a tradition that has survived up until the present moment. I intend to explore its geographical boundaries in my future research.

Looking backward has been a large part of the research presented here.

Present-day curing has been compared to that of the recent past, as well as to colonial-period sources. The well-known cultural continuity and conservatism of Yucatec Mayas is evidenced in my research. A subtler, seemingly contradictory cultural blueprint also emerged: the traditional curers in Yucatan continue to incorporate new and nontraditional elements of practice and treatment into their healing repertoires without losing sight of the old ways. This ability to colonize some desirable new thing or idea and fit it into the existing cultural framework is not limited to curing; it is replicated in many, if not all, areas of Yucatecan culture. Yucatecans retain their traditions while at the same time selectively adding new elements from outside their culture. This ability to combine the old with the new may help to explain the persistence of Maya traditions in the face of centuries of conquest and acculturation.

It is difficult to say what the future of traditional Yucatecan medicine will be. It would be tragic were it to disappear within the next generation or so. The facts are that the youngest curer with whom I worked is in his forties, and I have not met any young apprentices who seem eager to carry the oral traditions of Yucatecan medicine into the future. The curers I have come to know are regarded with little respect. It is much more common for them to be derided as antiquated rustics or viewed with suspicion. The decline of the Maya gods, discussed by Redfield and Villa Rojas (1962:112, 126) and Redfield (1941:229–70), continues. At times during the course of this research I have had the eerie sensation of capturing onto paper information that would otherwise disappear, à la Franz Boas. In this frame of mind, the outlook for traditional curers and curing in Yucatan seems grim.

Any one of the curers I have come to know might interrupt at this point and say that one has to think positively. After all, their cultural heritage has survived in oral form for some time. In Yucatan, curing continues to evolve and serves the physical, emotional, and spiritual needs of the people. Traditional curers utilize alcohol, aspirin, antibiotics, and Vicks VapoRub, while medical doctors utilize traditional Maya plant remedies for fever and skin complaints.

In the United States, people continue to rediscover traditional remedies, and natural products of all kinds are increasingly popular. Ironically, almost any natural product is in fashion in our high-tech world (a backlash?), while in Yucatan the pills and needles of Western medicine are more fashionable than teas and herbal treatments. I believe that a middle ground or balance must be sought. Western medicine and ethnomedicine both have something to offer the world as we move into this century. More and more sustainable resource studies are being conducted in tropical forests of the world, as people realize just how much biological diversity we all stand to lose within the next fifty to one hundred years. Researchers would do well to adopt something of the open-mindedness that characterizes the curers I have come to know in Yucatan.

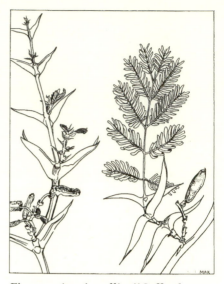

Figure 1. *Abrus precatorius* L.

Figure 2. *Acacia collinsii* Safford

Figure 3. *Apoplanesia
paniculata* Presl.

Figure 4. *Asclepias curassavica* L.

Figure 5. *Bauhinia divaricata* L.

Figure 6. *Blechum pyramidatum* (Juss.) Urban

Figure 7. *Bromelia pinguin* L.

Figure 8. *Bursera simaruba* (L.) Sargent

Figure 9. *Byrsonima crassifolia* (L.)
Kunth

Figure 10. *Calliandra grisebachii*
(Br. & Rose) Standley

Figure 11. *Cassia stenocarpa* Vogel

Figure 12. *Cassia villosa* Miller

Figure 13.
Catasetum maculatum Kunth

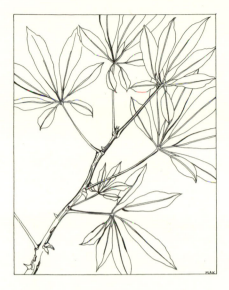

Figure 14. *Ceiba aesculifolia* (Kunth)
Britt. & Baker (Habit)

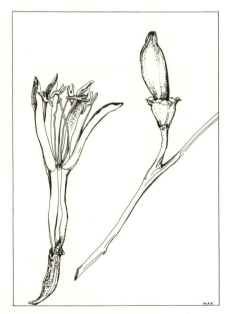

Figure 15. *Ceiba aesculifolia* (Kunth)
Britt. & Baker (Flower)

Figure 16. *Cnidoscolus chayamansa*
McVaugh

Figure 17. *Colubrina greggii* S. Watson

Figure 18. *Crataeva tapia* L.

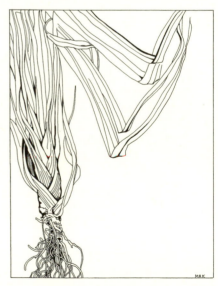

Figure 19. *Cydista potosina* (Schum & Loes) Loes

Figure 20. *Cymbopogon citratus* Stapf.

Figure 21.
Diphysa carthagenensis Jacq.

Figure 22.
Ehretia tinifolia L.

Figure 23.
Eupatorium odoratum L.

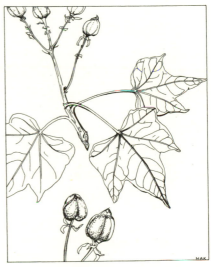

Figure 24.
Jatropha curcas L.

Figure 25.
Jatropha gaumeri Greenman

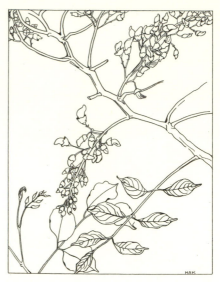

Figure 26. *Lonchocarpus longistylus*
Pittier

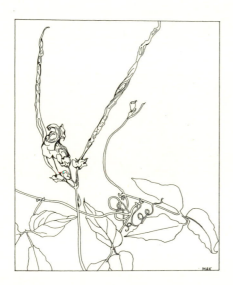

Figure 27. *Phaseolus elegans* Piper

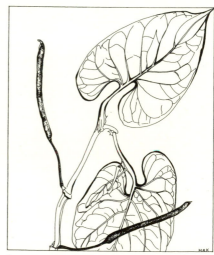

Figure 28. *Piper auritum* L.

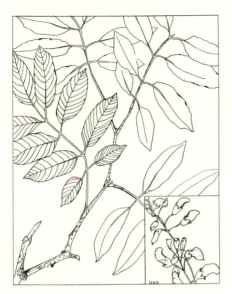

Figure 29. *Piscidia piscipula* (L.)
Sargent

Figure 30. *Plantago major* L.

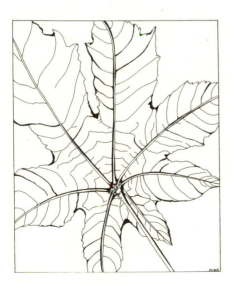

Figure 31. *Ricinus communis* L.

Figure 32. *Sida acuta* Burm.

Figure 33. *Talinum paniculatum* (Jacq.) Gaertn.

Figure 34. *Talinum triangulare* (Jacq.) Willd.

Figure 35. *Thouinia paucidentata* Radlk.

Figure 36. *Urera caracasana* (Jacq.) Griseb.

APPENDIX A

Plant Catalog

Abrus precatorius L.   Leguminosae
Mayan name: *oxoh*   Spanish name: *coral negro del monte*
See figure 1.
Field Notes: Vine with yellow flowers appearing in August. The seeds are small and bright red with a black point at one end, thus resembling small eyes. **Uses:** 1) To cure *ojo* (evil eye, which manifests itself as diarrhea) in children. Toss leaves into bath water. 2) Seeds can be strung into a necklace.

Roys (1931:296) as *xoco-ak:* Notes that the seeds are poisonous and that the leaves and roots have a licorice flavor.

Abutilon permolle (Willd.) Sweet   Malvaceae
Mayan name: *sac misib*
Field Notes: Shrub with yellow flowers in January. Grows to one meter tall. **Uses:** 1) To cure *fogajes* (rashes, eruptions) in children's mouths. 2) Branches are used as brooms.

Roys (1931:305): *Abutilon trisulcatum* (Jacq.) Urban as *zac-mizbil,* and *Ageratum gaumeri* Millsp. as *zac-mizib.* No uses are given for the first plant; the second is used externally to cure skin complaints and taken internally to accelerate parturition.

Acacia collinsii Safford   Leguminosae
Mayan name: *subin, subim*   Spanish name: *cuernero, cuerno de carnero*
See figure 2.
Field Notes: Shrub with yellow flowers. One to two meters tall. **Uses:** 1) To cure rheumatism. Venom from the ants that live in the plant is the medicine. Place an ant on affected area and let it bite you. 2) A drink of water in which you have washed nine ant larvae is secretly given to a cuckolded man to make him aware of his situation.

Roys (1931:312): *Acacia cornigera* (L.) Willd., *Acacia globulifera* Safford, as *zubin, zubin-che, cornezuelo.* Used for abdominal complaints.

Ageratum conyzoides L.   Compositae
Mayan name: *x holom x al*
Field Notes: Herb with purple-blue flowers, grows to one-half meter tall. **Uses:** To cure night fevers in nursing women caused by *ojo de agua.* Boil one-half kilo of whole plants in a bucket (ten liters) of water. Three consecutive days of baths are prescribed.

Roys (1931:284, 305): *A. conyzoides* L. (*Ageratum gaumeri* Millsp.) as *x-ta-ulum, x-ta-ulumil,* and *zac-mizib,* respectively. The first two names apply to a plant used to treat skin complaints, and the last is taken internally to hasten childbirth and used externally for skin complaints.

Annona glabra L.   Annonaceae
Mayan Name: *op*   Spanish Name: *annona*
Field Notes: Large tree, with round yellow fruit. The interior of the fruit is white, with shiny black seeds. **Uses:** 1) The fruit is edible. 2) The leaves are suspended above doorways to keep infections from entering the house.

Roys (1931:263) as *h-maak:* The fruit is edible, and when crushed it is a remedy for hiccoughs. The wood was used to cork bottles.

Annona squamosa L.   Annonaceae
Mayan Name: *tsalmuy*   Spanish name: *saramuyo* (The Spanish
                                                          name is a corruption of the Maya.)
Field Notes: Tree. Grows to five meters tall. The fruit is green, with white pulp and black seeds. **Uses:** 1) Edible fruit. 2) To cure *catarro* (head cold). Boil fifteen of the most tender leaves in a liter of water. The same drink also cures heartburn.

Roys (1931:313–14) as *tsalmuy:* Used for chills, fever. Fruit is edible.

Anthurium sp.   Araceae
Mayan Name: *x buc tum*
Field Notes: Described as a shrub. Grows to one meter tall. Large, shiny leaves and large red flowers in April. **Uses:** Purgative. The plant is combined with *Eupatorium odoratum* L., a *Cyperus* sp., and a liter of water. The medicine is drunk over a period of three days to pass urine.

Roys (1931:218): *Anthurium tetragonum* var. *yucatanensis* Engl., as *box kutz* ("black tobacco?"). No use is noted.

Apoplanesia paniculata Presl.   Leguminosae
Mayan name: *kik che*
See figure 3.
Field Notes: Tree. Said to have no flowers. **Uses:** 1) To cure hemorrhoids. Boil four thirty-centimeter pieces of bark with six liters of water until medicine is blood colored. Chill, then have patient sit in liquid for one hour. Take treatment four times a day until cured. 2) Dysentery. Drink nine drops of resin from trunk in a small glass of water. One treatment.

Roys (1931:239) as *chulul:* Mentions only the tensile strength of the wood.

Asclepias curassavica L.   Asclepiadaceae
Mayan name: *x anal* See figure 4.
Field Notes: Herb, one to two meters tall. The flowers are red and orange. **Uses:** To cure toothache. Apply sap from five leaves to each cavity. Each treatment lasts an hour.

Roys (1931:215) as *anal-kak, anal-xiu, cancerillo:* For abscesses of the breast.

Astrocasia phyllanthoides Rob. & Millsp.   Euphorbiaceae
Mayan Name: *x kah yuc*
Field Notes: Shrub, with white flowers and trumpet-shaped fruit. **Uses:** Used to

treat *granos* (pimples). Equal parts of this plant and *Calea urticifolia* (Mill.) DC. are boiled in a bucket of water. The affected area is bathed with the medicine.

Roys (1931:249) as *kah-yuc, ppix-thon-kax:* No use is given here, but on p. 84, the fruit of this plant is said to resemble that of another, called *ix-camuk-olal,* which is used in treating a type of irritability called "evil."

Bauhinia divaricata L. — Leguminosae
Mayan name: *u y oc wacax* Spanish name: *pata de vaca*
See figure 5.
Field Notes: Tree, to three meters tall. Flowers are pinkish-white, and the shape of the leaves resembles a cloven hoof. **Uses:** 1) To treat diabetes. Drink tea made with sixty grams of leaves boiled with a liter of water every day. 2) To cure sore throat "when blood comes up" (Don Tomás). 3) To cure constipation in children. Make a tea with thirty centimeters of root and a liter of water. Give four teaspoonfuls every three hours.

Roys (1931:315) as *tsulub-tok:* Multiple uses including treatment of fever, pleurisy, swollen head, neck, and breast. Flowers and roots are used to treat dysentery.

Bixa orellana L. — Bixaceae
Mayan name: *kiwi, kuxub* Spanish name: *achiote*
Field Notes: Tree with white flowers. The fruit is covered with brown bristles and contains small red seeds. Grows to three meters tall. **Uses:** 1) Measles. Drink water boiled with seeds and then cooled. Also, throw seeds under hammock to dispel disease. 2) Ground seeds used as a condiment. 3) Fresh seeds used as paint.

Roys (1931:260) as *kuxub, achiote, arnotto:* Leaves are used as a remedy for dysentery, and what is "probably erysipelas." The pulp is used for treating hemorrhoids, and the seeds are used as a condiment. On p. 143, the plant is described as a treatment for hive-like eruptions of the skin. On p. 234, it is combined with *chacah* (*Bursera simaruba* L.) to treat burns from *chechem* (*Metopium brownei* [Jacq.] Urban).

Blechum pyramidatum (Juss.) Urban — Acanthaceae
Mayan name: *x akab xiu, xaka xiu* Spanish name: *yierba de la noche*
See figure 6.
Field Notes: Vine with white flowers in April and May. **Uses:** To cure "night sweats" in children. Boil a handful in five liters of water for one-half hour. Cool, and wash baby two or three times with medicine.

Roys (1931:214): Used for coughs, bleeding, chills, and fever.

Borreria laevis (Lam.) Griseb. — Rubiaceae
Mayan Name: *menta kax*
Field Notes: Herb with small flowers and black fruit. **Uses:** Used to treat vomiting in children. The plant (unspecified part) is boiled with a half-liter of water, and

the medicine is administered in three-tablespoon doses every three hours.

Roys (1931:270, 284): The older synonyms for *B. laevis* (Lam.) Griseb. (*Spermacoce verticillata* L.) (*S. tenuior* L.) are called *ni-zotz* and *x-ta-ulmil,* respectively. No use is provided for either plant.

Borreria pulchra Millsp.   Boraginaceae
Mayan Name: *bacal che, baca che*

Field Notes: Large tree with white flowers and round, green fruit. **Uses:** The bark is crushed between the fingers and the aroma inhaled to stop nosebleeds. The bark of *Cedrela mexicana* is used the same way.

Roys (1931:215, 250) as *bacal-che, kak-che, kakal-che:* Used for treatment of fever, loss of speech, and (pp. 250, 180) "the dust of decayed tree trunk is applied to a specific type of skin irritation which resembles a burn." On p. 86, Roys suggests that "loss of speech" may be epilepsy.

Bromelia pinguin L.   Bromeliaceae
Mayan name: *ch'om*   Spanish name: *piñuela*
See figure 7.

Field Notes: Terrestrial plant, grows to one meter tall. Red and white flowers appear in March and April. **Uses:** 1) To staunch the flow of blood. Apply resin from leaves. 2) Dried, ground seeds mixed with yellow corn, honey, and water are fermented for fifteen days and distilled to make an alcoholic beverage.

Roys (1931:238): The common name for *Karatas plumiere* E. Mart. is *chom.* On p. 313, *B. pinguin* L. as *piñuela, piñuelilla,* and *tzalbay.* The fruit is a cure for tape-worms.

Brosimum alicastrum Swartz.   Moraceae
Mayan Name: *ox*   Spanish Name: *ramón*

Field Notes: Tree with white flowers and round fruit that resembles that of *Byrsonima crassifolia.* **Uses:** 1) The fruit is edible. It may be ground and eaten mixed with maize (like a filler?). 2) The resin of the branches is used to treat coughs. Five drops of resin are taken in hot water.

Roys (1931:272) as *ox, ramón:* The fruit is edible, and the sap is noted as a remedy for asthma, coughs, and phthisis.

Bunchosia swartziana Griseb.   Malpighiaceae
Mayan name: *sip che*

Field Notes: Tree with yellow flowers and small, round, red fruit. Grows to two meters tall. **Uses:** 1) To cure *vientos malos.* Hit person nine times with branches. 2) The above rite is performed after traditional ceremonies to disperse evil winds.
Roys (1931:309) *B. swartziana* Griseb. (*Bunchosia glandulosa* [Cav.] DC.) as *zip-ché:* Leaves are noted as a remedy for pleurisy, convulsions. They are applied directly for the former illness, while for the latter, a bundle of leaves is dipped in water and sprinkled on the patient, who is also bathed with an infusion of the same. Convulsions are seen as a product of evil winds. In addition, the plant is noted as a

remedy for "scab" although no mention is made of its well-known religious and magical uses.

Bursera simaruba (L.) Sarg.   Burseraceae
Mayan name: *chacah* See figure 8.
Field Notes: Tree, with yellow flowers in January. Grows to five meters tall. **Uses:** 1) To cure skin allergies (including reaction to *Metopium brownei*). Soak a large bunch of mashed leaves in a bucket of water for thirty minutes, then bathe affected areas. 2) For snakebite. Soak a sixty-centimeter piece of bark in one liter of water. Drink one-third of medicine three times a day for two days. Same medicine taken in same dosage cures fever.

Roys (pp. 227–28): Multiple uses include the following: The fruit is eaten to cure diarrhea, the leaves are used in the treatment of fevers and a variety of skin complaints such as sores, swellings, and rashes. The fruit and shoots are used for snakebite. Notes that tree can grow up to eighty-five feet tall.

Byrsonima bucidaefolia Standley   Malpighiaceae
Mayan Name: *sac pah*
Field Notes: Tree, grows to three or four meters tall. Flowers are yellow-orange, arranged in racemes. The fruit is round and white. Said to resemble *Byrsonima crassifolia*. **Uses:** Edible fruit.

Not in Roys, but on p. 306 *B. crassifolia* as *zac-pah:* Edible fruit. Used in treatment of asthma and coughs.

Byrsonima crassifolia (L.) Kunth   Malpighiaceae
Mayan name: *chi*   Spanish name: *nance*
See figure 9.
Field Notes: Tree with red flowers and small yellow fruit. Grows to ten meters tall. *Chi* means "mouth" in Yucatec, and each fruit is bite-sized. **Uses:** 1) Edible fruit. 2) To cure dysentery, boil thirty centimeters of bark in a liter of water. Drink one-third of the liquid each day for three days. Gargling with same cures sores in the mouth.

Roys (1931:306) as *zac-pah:* An infusion is drunk for coughs and a decoction is used as a bath for asthma. See also p. 10.

Caesalpinia gaumeri Greenm.   Leguminosae
Mayan name: *citan che*
Field Notes: Shrub with yellow flowers in January. Grows to "many meters tall" (Don Pedro). **Uses:** To prevent body odor. Leaves are rubbed under arms.

Roys (1931:225): Cures convulsions, aching bones, and "peccary bite." Tree is said to smell like a peccary. The translation of the Mayan name would be "pig tree" or "peccary tree." After reading Roys on this plant, I asked the curer who showed it to me if he had been playing a joke on me by giving its use as a deodorant, but he swore he had been telling the truth!

Calea urticifolia (Mill.) DC.   Compositae
Mayan Name: *x kah xicin*
Field Notes: Shrub with yellow flowers. **Uses:** Used in combination with *Cyperus ochraceus* Vahl to treat pimples. Equal parts of the plants are boiled in a bucket of water and the affected areas are washed with the medicine when cooled.

Roys (1931:295) as *xicin, yerba de la paloma:* Leaves and juice are used for "swollen scalp" and cacochymy of the skin.

Calliandra grisebachii (Br. & Rose) Standley   Leguminosae
Mayan name: *x mex nuxib, x mex nuxih*   Spanish name: *bigote grande*
See figure 10.
Field Notes: Shrub with white flowers in spring. Grows to three meters tall. **Uses:**
1) To cure *ojo de agua.* Boil one-meter section of leaves and stems in a liter of water, cool, and drink. Same medicine cures children who have been given evil eye, and so have one eye bigger than the other.

Roys (1931:265): *mex-nuxib* is identified as *Clematis dioica* L. Root is said to have astringent properties.

Callicarpa acuminata Kunth   Verbenaceae
Mayan name: *x pukim*
Field Notes: Shrub with white flowers and fruit. Grows to two meters tall. **Uses:** 1) To cure diarrhea and vomiting. Soak a bunch of leaves in cold water with a little sugar. Drink daily until cured.

Roys (1931:306) as *zac-puc-yim:* Describes plant as a tall shrub with white flowers and black fruit.

Capsicum annuum var. *aviculare* (Dierb.) D'Arcy & Eshbaugh   Solanaceae
Mayan Name: *max ic*   Spanish Name: *chile max*
Field Notes: White flowers, small fruit. Very spicy fruit.
Uses: Edible fruit. Said to be hotter than *habanero* chiles. These or *habaneros* are ground up and applied to sores, a treatment that must be quite painful.

Roys (1931:247) *as ic, yax-ic:* Notes that the plant is often combined with other ingredients in treatments. *Max-ic* is described as a wild variety "like grains of wheat" (in size). Used for an impressive number of medical problems including: phthisis, delayed parturition, diarrhea and cramps, "vomiting blood," and giddiness.

Carica papaya L.   Caricaceae
Mayan Name: *ch'ich' put*   Spanish Name: *papaya de pájaros, papaya silvestre*
Field Notes: Tree, with small flowers and fruits. The fruit of this papaya is said to "grow in racemes," while the cultivated papaya fruits "hang separately" (Don Pedro). **Uses:** The resin is applied to snakebites.

Roys (1931:280) as *put, chich-put:* Fruit is edible. Plant is used in the treatment of assorted swellings. The root is used for skin eruptions.

Casimiroa tetrameria Millsp.   Rutaceae
Mayan Name: *yuy*
Field Notes: Tree, grows to three to four meters tall. Flowers are white and fruit is round and green, "like *guayas.*" **Uses:** The leaves are applied to the patient's chest with Vicks VapoRub to "draw the fever within" (Don Tomás).

 Roys (1931:301) as *yuy, h-yuy:* Notes that the tree is rare. The leaves are used to treat asthma and "diarrhea accompanied by chills." For treating the latter illness, the patient is seated over a pot of the steaming leaves.

Cassia atomaria L.   Leguminosae
Mayan Name: *x tu habin, x tu habim*
Field Notes: Tree, grows to three meters tall. Yellow flowers in the dry season. The fruits are green, turning black as they mature. **Uses:** Crushed leaves are inhaled to stop nosebleeds. See also entries for *Cedrela mexicana* and *Borreria pulchra,* which are used similarly.

 Roys (1931:287) *C. atomaria* L. (*Cassia emarginata* L.) as *x-tu-ab, x-tu-habin:* The plant is described as "very heating" and is prescribed for chills or convulsions ("cold" conditions). See also p. 199.

Cassia stenocarpa Vogel   Leguminosae
Mayan name: *x ocen kab*   Spanish name: *llanto de miel*
See figure 11.
Field Notes: Herb, one to two meters tall. **Uses:** To cure *llanto* (crying) in children. Grind fresh leaves and use to draw a cross on child's forehead, then place a whole plant under child's hammock. Not in Roys.

Cassia villosa Miller   Leguminosae
Mayan name: *sal che*   See figure 12.
Field Notes: Shrub with yellow flowers in January. Grows to two meters tall. **Uses:** To cure *manchas blancas* (white stains or spots on the skin). Pack leaves on affected areas. Three treatments.

 Roys (1931:308) as *zal che:* Notes that ringworm is called *zal.* The name would then translate as "ringworm tree."

Catasetum sp.   Orchidaceae
Mayan Name: *ch'it cuc*
Field Notes: Parasitic vine that grows in forks of trees. **Uses:** Apply ground, roasted fruit to external tumors. Draws infections.

Catasetum maculatum Kunth   Orchidaceae
Mayan Name: *ch'it cuc*   Spanish name: *platanillo*
See figure 13.
Field Notes: Parasitic vine with greenish-yellow flowers. **Uses:** To heal sores. Cook fruit whole in hearth ashes for one hour, then apply to affected area. Two treatments.

 Roys (1931:237) as *chit-kuk, chit-cuuc:* Used as a poultice, which causes abscesses to open.

Cecropia peltata L.   Moraceae
Mayan name: *koch*   Spanish name: *guarumbo*
Field Notes: Tree, with white flowers that bloom beginning in August. Grows to ten meters tall. **Uses:** 1) To treat diabetes. Boil four or five leaves in one liter of water. Drink daily. 2) Leaves can be dried, chopped, and rolled to make cigarettes. 3) Stems used to be used as irrigation pipes.

Roys (1931:256): The older name for *C. peltata* L. (*Cecropia obtusa* Trecul.) as *x-coch-le:* a remedy for retention of urine. On p. 39, it is noted as a cure for "bloody flux."

Cedrela mexicana M. Roem   Meliaceae
                                                        Spanish name: *cedro*
Field Notes: Tree with cream-colored flowers in February. Said to grow many meters tall. **Uses:** 1) To stop nosebleeds. Inhale the aroma of crushed leaves. 2) To cure earache. Chop a five-centimeter square section of bark, wrap in cloth and heat. Then squeeze a few drops of resin in ear. 3) Wood is used for house and furniture construction.

Roys (1931:258) as *kuche, kulche:* Leaves cure earache, dysentery. Gum is used for toothache, and wood is used to build ships.

Ceiba aesculifolia (Kunth) Britt. & Baker   Bombacaceae
Mayan name: *yax che*   Spanish name: *pochote, ceiba*
See figures 14 (Habit) and 15 (Flower)
Field Notes: Tall tree with palmate leaves and purple flowers. **Uses:** Juice from fruit is drunk as a general tonic. It is said that if boys play with the fruit, they will grow breasts. Ethnographers Redfield and Villa Rojas (1962:19, 34, 207) note that the *ceiba* tree is the haunt of the *x-tabai* (a mythical seductress who causes madness or death in her prey) after dark and that if little girls play with the fruit their breasts will grow too large.

Roys (1931:277): States that the word *pochote* comes from the Nahuatl and that the tree is also known as *choo.* On p. 24, it is noted as a treatment for snakebite, and on p. 105, as a treatment for "fainting." P. 238 mentions the use of the plant as a remedy for fever

Chlorophora tinctoria (L.) Gaud.   Moraceae
                                                        Spanish name: *mora*
Field Notes: Tree, grows to ten meters tall. Flowers are yellowish green.
Uses: To remove teeth painlessly. Apply resin with a piece of cotton. Do not touch other teeth. Not in Roys.

Cissus rhombifolia Vahl   Vitaceae
Mayan Name: *x tab canil, x ta canih*
Field Notes: Vine, with white flowers that turn yellow as they dry. The fruit is round and purple. **Uses:** To "catch" witches. The vine is draped over doorways and serves as a trap if witches attempt to enter the house in animal form.

Roys (1931:281) as *tab-can, x-tab-canil:* Notes use of young shoots for snakebite and use of the crushed root for skin complaints. On p. 199, the plant is mentioned as part of a remedy for "suppression of urine in a horse." See also p. 23, for another reference to the use of the plant for snakebite.

Cissus sicyoides L.   Vitaceae
Mayan Name: *x tab canil, x ta canih*
Field Notes: Vine, with small clusters of white-yellow flowers. The fruit is round and black (dark purple?), appearing in January and February. **Uses:** Form crosses out of the vine and suspend over doorways to prevent witches from entering. "They can suck your blood if they get in" (Don Cósimo).

Roys (1931:281): *C. rhombifolia* Vahl as *tab-can, x-tab-canil*. See previous entry. I collected two *Cissus* species while working with the same curer. He assigned the same Maya name and use to both of them. On p. 300, *C. sicyoides* has the Maya name of *yax-tab-canil*. On p. 306, it is noted as a treatment for skin complaints, buboes, and retention of urine.

Citrus aurantifolia (Christm.) Swingle   Rutaceae
Spanish Name: *limón*
Field Notes: Tree, grows to four meters tall. White flowers and yellow-green fruit. The smallest and bitterest variety of limes are referred to as *indios*. **Uses:** 1) As a skin treatment. Bury a whole fruit in the hearth ashes until soft. Wash face with fruit to "rejuvenate" it and remove "stains." 2) The juice (of a whole fruit if small, one-half fruit if large) is drunk before breakfast as a tonic for the libido. 3) Drink the juice of (quantity unspecified) fruits as an antidote for poison. Not in Roys.

Citrus aurantium L.   Rutaceae
Mayan Name: *pakal*   Spanish Name: *naranjo agrío* (refers to tree),
naranja agría (refers to fruit)
Field Notes: Tree, grows to five meters tall. White flowers in July and again in February. *Uses:* 1) A tea made from the leaves is taken to increase appetite and treat vomiting. 2) Scrapings from the peel are mixed with a gram of salt and applied to bruises. 3) To treat *bilis*. A quarter-liter of juice is mixed with one-eighth liter of water and three grams of salt. This medicine is taken before breakfast every day. Roys (1931:249): *Citrus amara* Link as *kahpakal*, literally "sour orange." No use is given here, but on p. 273 *C. aurantium* as *Chuhuc pakal*, literally "sweet orange." (But *Citrus sinensis* is the sweet orange?) *Pakal* is the general term in Maya for "orange." Uses include treatment for coughs, asthma, spitting blood, toothache, and buboes. For the latter condition, the pulp is applied to the affected area. Also, on p. 313, *zutz-pakal* (sour orange) is mentioned as a treatment for colic.

Cnidoscolus chayamansa McVaugh   Euphorbiaceae
See figure 16.   Spanish name: *chay, chaya*
Field Notes: Shrub, with yellow flowers in July. Grows to two meters tall. **Uses:** 1) Edible leaves. A pleasant tea is made from one-half kilo of leaves boiled with one liter of water and is taken as a general tonic. 2) A small dose of the sap from the leaves is drunk daily as a purgative. It "cleans out" the kidney and the bladder.

Roys (1931:234) *chay, chinchin-chay, tzintzin-chay, x-tzah* as *Cnidoscolus aconitifolius* (Mill.) I. M. Johnston (*Jatropha aconitifolia* Mill.): This is described as an edible plant with various uses, including as an aid to parturition and as a remedy for biliousness and jaundice. These uses may be based on the purgative qualities of the plant. On p. 137, *chaya* is identified as *Jatropha urens* (L.), which is used in the treatment of "a certain small ulcer," but in the index (1931:322) *tzintzin-chay, chinchin-chay* as "*Jatropha urens stimulosa* Mich.) Muell. (?)" McVaugh separated the edible from the stinging species post-Roys.

Coccoloba uvifera L.

Polygonaceae
Spanish name: *uva del mar*

Field Notes: Vine-like tree that grows near the sea. The leathery leaves are round and the fruit looks like grapes. **Uses:** 1) The fruit is edible. 2) To cure diarrhea. Boil five pieces of bark in one liter of water for fifteen minutes. Drink. 3) To cure ulcers. Add fifty grams of alcohol to the above tea after it has cooled. Three spoonfuls before each meal for three days, then rest eight days and repeat.

Roys (1931:270) as *nii-che, uva del mar:* Fruit is edible. The pulp is used as remedy for sore eyes.

Colubrina greggii S. Watson
See figure 17.

Rhamnaceae
Spanish name: *balsamo de los Mayas*

Field Notes: Tree with yellow flowers in January. The green fruit appears in February. Grows to two meters tall. **Uses**: Pain killer. Cures body aches. Boil bark scrapings in a glass of water, then rub on affected area.

Roys (1931:279) as *puc-yim, pucim:* Multiple uses. Plant is a remedy for coughs, asthma, abscesses and ulcers, and granulated eyelids. On p. 6 the plant is mentioned in a remedy for phthisis, and on p. 64 as a treatment for "blood vomit."

Cordia sp.
Mayan Name: *kop te*

Boraginaceae
Spanish Name: *siricote*

Field Notes: Tree with yellow trumpet-shaped flowers and round fruit that turns from green to yellow at maturity. **Uses:** 1) Edible fruit. 2) Dried leaves may be used to scrub wood and wash dishes. 3) Wood is excellent for furniture construction.

Roys lists five species of *Cordia,* of which two have similar common names; *C. dodecandra* A.DC. as *kopté, chac-kopté. C. sebestena* as *zac-kopté.* See next entry.

Cordia dodecandra A.DC.
Mayan Name: *kop te*

Boraginaceae
Spanish Name: *siricote*

Field Notes: Tree, grows to three or four meters tall. Orange flowers. The fruit turns from green to yellow at maturity. **Uses:** 1) The fruit is edible. 2) The fibrous leaves can be used fresh or dried to scour pots.

Roys (pp. 257–58) as *kopté, chac-kopté:* Fruit is described as greenish or yellowish. *Cordia sebestena* L. (1931:305) as *zac-kopté, siricote blanco,* and *anacahuite.* Fruit is edible.

Crataeva tapia L.   Capparidaceae
See figure 18.   Spanish name: *tres marías*
Field Notes: Shrub, with yellow flowers in February. Grows to three meters tall. Three leaflets to each leaf, hence the name. **Uses:** To cure headache. Chop leaves, plaster on forehead, and bind with a piece of cloth. Leave in place until cured.

Roys (1931:257) as *kolok-max:* "Some unspecified part, perhaps the leaf" is used on infected gums. Notes that fruit resembles a small lemon. Tree grows to twenty meters tall. See also p. 185, where the name *tres marías* appears.

Croton cortesianus Kunth   Euphorbiaceae
Mayan Name: *sac xiu*
Field Notes: Shrub with white flowers and small round fruit, "like *hol*" *(Hampea integerrima)* (Don Pedro). Undersides of the leaves are silvery white. **Uses:** Used to treat measles and smallpox. Leaves are boiled and the patient is bathed with the medicine.

Roys (1931:240) as *ek-balam:* The root is used to treat diarrhea, and the gum or bark is employed in the treatment of "sliver in the foot" on p. 204.

Croton flavens L.   Euphorbiaceae
Mayan Name: *xicin burro, xicim burro*   Spanish Name: *orejón del burro*
Field Notes: Shrub, grows to one meter tall. The leaves are shaped much like a donkey's ear and are covered with dense, velvety hair. Fruit is small and green. **Uses:** The resin in the leaves is applied to the corners of the mouth to cure "whitish infections" (cold sores?) (Don Pedro). Apply once or twice, until healed.

Roys (1931:293) as *xabalam:* On p. 24, it is mentioned as a treatment for snakebite, and on p. 72, it is prescribed for "chills accompanied by diarrhea." See also p. 240 for confusion between this species and *C. cortesianus* Kunth.

Croton humilis L.   Euphorbiaceae
Mayan name: *x ic aban, hic aban*
Field Notes: Shrub, grows to one meter tall. White flowers in December. **Uses:** 1) To dissolve warts. Open warts and apply resin from the stem. Three treatments. 2) To get rid of fleas, sweep floor with branches. Plant causes blindness when ingested by cattle. It is used as an insecticide in Jamaica.

Roys (1931:247) as *ic-aban:* Leaves used on ulcers, juice from plant used on syphilitic sores. See also p. 161, another reference to treatment of buboes.

Croton miradorensis Muell. Arg.   Euphorbiaceae
Mayan name: *xicin burro, xicim burro*   Spanish name: *orejón del burro*
Field Notes: Shrub, grows to one meter tall. Leaves are covered in a dense pubescence, hence the name "donkey's ear." **Uses:** To cure "whitish infections in the corners of the mouth" (Don Pedro). Apply resin. See also *Croton flavens* (same use). Not in Roys.

Cydista potosina (Schum. & Loes.) Loes.   Bignoniaceae
Mayan name: *x ek ixil, x ek ixih* See figure 19.
Field Notes: Vine with white flowers in spring. **Uses:** 1) To staunch the flow of blood.
Chew up six leaves and apply to wound. One curer uses bark scrapings for the
same purpose. 2) To tie up house-poles. 3) To cure head colds. Boil equal parts of
the plant with *pata de vaca (Bauhinia divaricata)* and *flor del roble (Ehretia tinifolia*
?). Drink four teaspoons every two hours for five days.

     Roys (1931:241) *Bignonia unguis-cati* as *x-ek-kixil,* or *ek-kixil-ak:* This "cooling"
vine is used as a treatment for swellings, sores, and eruption of pustules.

Cymbopogon citratus Stapf.   Gramineae
See figure 20.   Spanish name: *zacate limón*
Field Notes: Herb, grows to one-half meter tall. The leaves are grayish-green. Plant
is said not to have fruit or flowers. The plant is known as "fever-grass" in the West
Indies. In Brazil it is dried and used to scent clothing stored in closets or trunks.
Uses: 1) To improve appetite. Make a tea with five stalks per liter of water. 2) Above
tea cures colic. Not in Roys.

Cyperus sp.   Cyperaceae
Mayan Name: *x tu put su'uc*
Field Notes: Herb with tiny flowers. **Uses:** 1) Used to treat hiccoughs. Boil chopped root
in a liter of water, and drink. 2) Put washed pieces of roots in trunks to scent clothing.
Not in Roys. Compare with information on other *Cyperus* species in next entry.

Cyperus ochraceus Vahl   Cyperaceae
Mayan Name: *x cambal xan, x camba xan*
Field Notes: Small herb with green flowers. **Uses:** The roots of this plant are boiled
with those of *x cambal hau (Dorstenia contrajerva)* to treat infertility in women.
The tea is taken two times each day.

     Roys (1931:264) as *mazcab-zuuc,* which is translated as "copper-grass": No use
is given. On p. 227, *C. uncinnatus* Poir. as *x-chab-xan* (with a question mark after
this name) and a suggestion that *x-cabal-xaan* may have been intended.

Dalea nutans (Cav.) Willd.   Leguminosae (Papilionoideae)
Mayan Name: *chac motz*
Field Notes: Small herb, with reddish roots, and distinctive glandular spots on the
leaves. The flowers resemble those of *x mudz (Mimosa pudica).* Dehiscent fruits
turn from green to black at maturity. **Uses:** Used to make a dye. The roots must be
washed, cut, and boiled to release the pigment. Yields a pinkish dye.

     Roys (1931:230): *Sicydium tamnifolium* Kunth as *chac-motz.* No use is given
for this plant.

Diphysa carthagenensis Jacq.   Leguminosae
Mayan name: *dzudzuc* See figure 21.

Field Notes: Shrub with yellow flowers in January and May. Grows to five meters tall. **Uses:** 1) To cure evil eye in children. Bathe child's face and touch with leaves. 2) To cure dysentery "when one is passing a lot of blood" (Don Cósimo). Boil a thirty-centimeter section in one liter of water. Drink it gradually over the course of the day. Repeat until cured.

Roys (1931:316) as *tsutsuc, x-tsutsuc:* Crushed leaves are applied to inflamed eyes, abscesses, and ruptures. An infusion of leaves is taken for dysentery.

Dorstenia contrajerva L.   Moraceae
Mayan name: *cambal hau, camba hau*
Field Notes: Plant is a small herb with green leaf-like flowers. Common around ruins. **Uses:** To cure colic. Boil two roots (only the middle section is used) in two small glasses of water. Drink tepid. Use one-half root for children.

Roys (1931:222) as *x-cambal-hau:* Multiple uses, including as a treatment for colds, dysentery, and diarrhea. The plant and its root are an antidote for poison and a cure for skin ailments. See also p. 6 (remedy for colds) and p. 22 (remedy for spider bite).

Ehretia tinifolia L.   Boraginaceae
Mayan Name: *bec* See figure 22.   Spanish Name: *roble*
Field Notes: Tall shrub with white flowers in April, May, and June. **Uses:** To cure headache. Apply four or five leaves to forehead, and leave in place until dried.

Roys (1931:217) as *beec.* The plant is a remedy for ulcers, and has edible fruit.

Elytraria imbricata (Vahl) Pers.   Acanthaceae
Mayan Name: *cambal xan*
Field Notes: A small herb that grows to one-half meter tall. Purple flowers in January. **Uses:** To hasten childbirth. Boil thirteen plants with fifteen centimeters of *pixoy (Guazuma ulmifolia)* bark in one-half liter of water. Drink warm, and baby will be born within one-half hour.

Roys (1931:221): *Elytraria imbricata* (Vahl.) Pers. (*Elytraria squamosa* [Jacq.] Lindau) as *x-cabal-xaan.* Multiple uses include remedy for dysentery, and "blood-vomit and liver complaints."

Erythrina standleyana Krukoff   Leguminosae
Mayan Name: *chac mol che*
Field Notes: Tree with red flowers in January. Grows to two meters tall. **Uses:** To clear eye infections. Mash seeds and squeeze a drop of resin in eye.

Roys (1931:230): *colorín* as *Erythrina americana* Mill.: Multiple uses. Leaf or fruit is used for treating eye complaints. Boiled leaves are applied to insect bites, and crushed fresh leaves are poulticed on abscesses. On p. 98, *E. coralloides* Mocq. & Sesse is used in a treatment for "piercing pain in a man's eye." Both of the species mentioned above are older synonyms for *E. standleyana* Krukoff.

Eupatorium odoratum L.   Compositae

Mayan Name: *x tok aban, x tok abam* See figure 23.

Field Notes: Shrub with white flowers. Grows one to two meters tall. **Uses:** Retention of urine. Boil two handfuls of *x buc tum* (*Anthurium* sp.) roots with equal parts of *x tok abam* (*Eupatorium odoratum*) and two small *x tu put su'uc* (*Cyperus* sp.) plants. Drink one liter of medicine over the course of three days to cure.

Roys (1931:286) *Eupatorium odoratum* L. (*Eupatorium conyzoides* Mill.) as *tok-aban:* Leaves are used to cure gonorrhea, malaria, ulcers, and blood in urine.

Euphorbia hypericifolia L.   Euphorbiaceae

Mayan Name: *xanab mucuy, xana mucuy*   Spanish Name: *zapatos de tortolas*

Field Notes: Herb with small white flowers in January. **Uses:** To pass stones. Boil a kilo of whole plants in three liters of water. Drink one bottle each day for three days.

Roys (1931:293) *Euphorbia hirta* L. as *yerba del pollo:* Staunches flow of blood, tumors, dysentery. Notes that the name *xanab-mucuy* is applied to a number of small, prostrate *Euphorbia* species. Throughout the text, *yerba de la golondrina* refers to *E. dioica* Kunth while *yerba del pollo* refers to *E. hirta.* It may be that the system of common names ascribes each species to a different bird.

Euphorbia schlechtendalii Boiss.   Euphorbiaceae

Mayan Name: *sac chacah*

Field Notes: Shrub, with white flowers in April or May. **Uses:** To cure pellagra. Boil one-meter-and-twenty-centimeter section in a bucket of water. Bathe patient, and repeat until cured.

Roys (1931:303) as *zac chacah:* Uses include as treatment for coughs, tumors, and scalp complaints. On p. 218 *box chacah* ("Black chacah") is identified as *Euphorbia gaumerii* Millsp.

Evolvulus alsiniodes Boiss.   Convolvulaceae

Mayan Name: *x puluc xom*

Field Notes: Herb with blue flowers and small green fruits. **Uses:** To treat headache. Apply the entire plant to forehead until it is dry.

Roys (1931:294) as *yax-xiu, x-yax-xiu:* No use noted.

Ficus sp.   Moraceae

Mayan Name: *copo*   Spanish Name: *alamo*

Field Notes: Tall tree with reddish-yellow flowers in June and July. Fruit is small and green with a pink interior. **Uses:** Resin is applied to umbilical cord to heal it.

Two *Ficus* species are noted in Roys: *F. cotinifolia* Kunth (1931:226), and *F. mexicanus* Miq. (1931:303). No medicinal uses are noted for the latter species. Uses for the former employ the milky juice of the plant in treating "abscess of the ear" and "sliver in the foot." On p. 97, *F. cotinifolia* Kunth is noted as a treatment for earache. None of the uses is similar to those recorded for *Ficus radula* Willd. (See next entry.)

Ficus radula Willd. Moraceae
Mayan Name: *akum*
Field Notes: Tall tree with round, green fruit with red interior. **Uses:** To control snoring. Placing a bunch under the sleeper's hammock solves the problem. Not in Roys.

Gossypium hirsutum L. Malvaceae
Mayan Name: *taman, tamam* Spanish Name: *mata de algodón*
Field Notes: Shrub, grows to two meters tall. Pink flowers in January. **Uses:** To cure coughs. Version #1—Soak or boil six to eight leaves per cup of water for ten minutes. Drink each day for a week if cough is bad. A little sugar improves taste. Version #2— Boil a handful of leaves with equal amounts of *naranjo agrío* and *saramuyo* leaves in one liter of water. Drink it warm, and avoid cold water or drinks the next day.

Roys (1931:282): Multiple uses. A decoction of the plant is a treatment for asthma, crushed leaves are poulticed on ulcers and various skin complaints, and flowers are applied to the genitals to cure venereal diseases. The seeds are taken for "tenesmus." It is mentioned as a cure for earache on p. 95.

Gouania sp. Rhamnaceae
Mayan Name: *om xiu*
Field Notes: Sprawling vine with white flowers in racemes in April and May. The fruit is small, green, and grows in clumps of three. **Uses:** 1) To cure rashes in the mouth. Leaves are boiled and the tea is used as a gargle when cooled. Three times daily. 2) To cure pimples. The above tea is used to wash the affected area once a day for four days.

Roys (1931:271): Lists *G. dominguensis* L. as *om-ak, x-om-ak,* which is used to treat sores in the mouth, as well as "blood vomit" and "rotten liver."

Guazuma ulmifolia Lam. Sterculiaceae
Mayan Name: *pixoy*
Field Notes: Tree with greenish flowers and round, black fruit. Grows to ten meters tall. **Uses:** To hasten delivery and lessen labor pain. Boil one-meter section bark in two liters of water for twenty minutes.

Roys (1931:276): A decoction is used to treat abdominal pains and retention of urine, while an infusion of crushed young shoots is employed for relief of cramps and diarrhea.

Hamelia patens Jacq. Rubiaceae
Mayan Name: *x kanan*
Field Notes: Shrub with orange flowers in July and January, and blue fruit in March and August. Grows to three meters tall. **Uses:** 1) To cure scrapes and welts. Boil two handfuls of leaves in a bucket of water. Wash affected area. 2) Juice from fruit makes a blue paint. 3) Boiled leaves (more than amount in first use) make a yellow paint.

Roys (1931:250): Fruit is described as red. Plant is used on swellings of the legs and scrapes. Crushed leaves are applied to scabs, while boiled leaves are used in a bath for asthma, coughs, snakebite, and fever. See also p. 14.

Hampea integerrima Schlechtendal   Malvaceae
Mayan Name: *hol*   Spanish Name: *agujero*
Field Notes: Tree, grows to a height of two meters. Small, round fruit "hangs like earrings" (Don Pedro). **Uses:** The fibrous bark is used to make ropes.

Roys (1931:245): *Hol* seems to be a generic name for *Hibiscus* species.

Helicteres barvensis Jacq.   Sterculiaceae
Mayan Name: *suput, sutup*
Field Notes: Tree, grows to three meters tall. Flowers are yellow, and fruits look "rolled." Serrated leaves. **Uses:** The fruit is used to make nonverbal young children speak. Place fruit in child's mouth and turn nine times. Only one treatment is necessary.

Roys (1931:313) as *zutup, tzutup:* Multiple uses listed, including as a cure for convulsions, giddiness, epilepsy, and coughs.

Hibiscus poeppigii (Sprengel) Garcke   Malvaceae
Mayan Name: *x tup kinil*
Field Notes: Herb, with red flowers. Round fruit, alternate leaves. **Uses:** The flowers are soaked in warm water. The medicine is applied three times a day for "swollen breasts."

Roys (1931:289): *Hibiscus poeppigii* (Sprengel) Garcke (*H. tubiflorus* DC.) is noted as *x-tup-kinil*. The flower or leaf is a remedy for earache. Another common name, *hol,* is given for the last-named synonym on p. 245.

Hymenocallis americana Roem.   Amaryllidae
                                                     Spanish Name: *lirio blanco*
Field Notes: White flowers, long bright green leaves. **Uses:** The roots (bulbs) are cooked in hearth ashes and applied to sores and external cancers. Poultice should be left in place until dried. *Catasetum maculatum* is used similarly. Not in Roys.

Hyptis sp.   Labiatae
Mayan Name: *chac sikin*
Field Notes: Erect herb, opposite leaves. Small white flowers. Strong scent when crushed. **Uses:** The leaves are soaked in water, and the tea is taken to treat stomach upsets, stomach pains, and vomiting.
Roys (1931:296): *Hyptis pectinata* (L.) Poit. and *H. suaveolens* (L.) Poit. as *xolté-x-nuc.* Used to treat dysentery, as well as "night-fevers," "especially in babies."

Indigofera suffruticosa Mill.   Leguminosae
Mayan Name: *ch'oh*
Field Notes: Shrub, grows to two meters tall. The flowers are yellow-orange. **Uses:** The fresh leaves are crushed and applied to insect bites. The poultice should be left in place until dried. I tried this remedy and found it effective, although it burned.

Roys (1931:238): *Indigofera suffruticosa* Mill. (*Indigofera anil* L.) as *choh.* Leaves are used to make a dye, and to treat convulsions.

Ipomoea tiliaceae (Willd.) Choisy   Convolvulaceae
Mayan Name: *yax ceiyli*
Field Notes: Vine with blue flowers in January. **Uses:** To relieve cramps. Boil one kilo
of leaves in one liter of water and bathe with the medicine once a day for three days.

Roys (1931:244): *Ipomoea tiliaceae* (Willd.) Choisy (*I. fastigiata* Sweet) is called
hebil. No use for the plant is given.

Jatropha curcas L.   Euphorbiaceae
Mayan Name: *ponpon che, ponpoche* See figure 24.
Field Notes: Shrub, grows to four meters tall. Said not to flower. **Uses:** To pass
stones. Drink a tiny glass of resin with an equal amount of water. One treatment.

Roys (1931:222, 309) as *x-cacal-che, zicilté, avellanas:* "A medicinal oil is extracted
from the fruit," but its use is not described further.

Jatropha gaumeri Greenman   Euphorbiaceae
Mayan Name: *pomol che* See figure 25.
Field Notes: Tree, grows to two meters tall. **Uses:** 1) Resin is applied to wound to
staunch bleeding. 2) To dissolve stones a tea is made by boiling a five-centimeter
section of root with four or five glasses of water. 3) Drink ten drops of resin in a
cup of water to cure diarrhea. Two treatments.

Roys (1931:278) as *x-pomol che:* The fruit is a purgative, the gum or roots are
used as a remedy for dysentery, the crushed leaves are used on skin complaints,
and an infusion of the gum is used against yellow fever. See also p. 49.

Kallstroemia maxima (L.) Torr. & Gray   Zygophyllaceae
Mayan Name: *chitun kax*
Field Notes: Sprawling herb, with yellow flowers and green fruit. Large central
root is white. **Uses:** The chopped leaves of the plant are applied fresh to treat spider
bites. Relieves pain.

Roys (1931:295): *Kallstroemia maxima* (L.) Torr. & Gray (*Tribulus maximus* L.)
as *xichil-ak* ("tendon-vine"). Although a use is perhaps suggested by the common
name, nothing more explicit is provided.

Lepidium virginicum L.   Brassicaceae
                                                           Spanish Name: *altanisa*
Field Notes: Herb, with small yellow/white flowers. I think that the informant
misidentified this plant. We were unable to locate another specimen. **Uses:** To
treat coughs. A small handful of leaves is boiled with a half-liter of water and is
taken as a tea.

Roys (1931:280) as *x-put-can, mastuerzo,* and pepper-grass. Said to smell like
papaya. The seeds are used as a remedy for flatulence, and the leaves are applied
to pustules, wounds, and cuts. On p. 15, it is noted as an aid in hastening delivery.

Leucaena leucocephala (Lam.) de Witt   Leguminosae
Mayan Name: *uaxim*
Field Notes: Tree, with white flowers and pod fruit that turns from green to black at maturity. **Uses:** People "from México" eat the seeds, which are said to contain "a lot of vitamins" (Don Pedro). However, if horses eat the leaves, it makes the hair of their tails fall out.

    Roys (pp. 291–92): *Leucaena leucocephala* (Lam.) de Witt (*Leucaena glauca* [L.] Benth.) as *uaxim*. The same effect on the tails of "any animal with a strong-haired tail" is noted. The young shoots are taken internally for insect bites, and an infusion of the leaves is taken for a disease "characterized by headache and pain in the heart." See also p. 147.

Lonchocarpus longistylus Pittier   Leguminosae
Mayan Name: *balche* See figure 26.
Field Notes: Tree with blue flowers in January, and green fruit in February and March. Grows to fifteen meters tall. **Uses:** To make ceremonial wine. Combine ten liters of water, three twenty-centimeter sections of bark, two liters of honey, and one kilo of fine-ground maize. Ferment at least three days and distill.

    Roys (1931:216): Describes the process of making and drinking the wine and notes its purgative effect. Crushed leaves are also rubbed on smallpox sores, and an infusion of them is employed in treating loss of speech.

Malmea depressa (Baillon) Fries   Annonaceae
Mayan Name: *elemuyil*
Field Notes: Tree with yellow flowers in February. Grows to ten meters tall. **Uses:** 1) To make a tonic for kidneys. Boil two small pieces of bark and root with one liter of water. Drink daily. 2) Above also helps to pass stones.
Roys (1931:241): *Malmea depressa* (Baillon) Fries (*Guatteria gaumeri* Greenman) as *ele-muy.* The author notes the use of the plant for treating skin afflictions in Spanish Yucatecan texts.

Melochia pyramidata L.   Sterculiaceae
Mayan Name: *x malva xiu*
Field Notes: Small herb has pinkish flowers with yellowish centers in January. **Uses:** To cure *pasmo* (chills, tetanus). Boil two thirty-centimeter bunches with one liter of water. Chill and drink one-half liter tepid each day for two days. Not in Roys, but on p. 303, *M. tomentosa* L. is called *zac-chichibe* and is used to treat swellings, buboes of the groin, fever, and to hasten childbirth.

Merremia dissecta (Jacq.) Hallier F.   Convolvulaceae
Mayan Name: *ha'as ak*
Field Notes: Vine, with palmate leaves. The fruit is green and pointed, resembling that of tomatillos, rather than bananas as the name suggests. **Uses:** To cure *tuch.* When the sun is setting, you touch the patient's belly button nine times to "make it go in" (Don Pedro).

Roys (1931:205, 247): *M. dissecta* (*Ipomoea sinuata* Ortega) as *hunab-tzotz*. The plant is used to treat seven unidentified diseases named for seven planets. Two vines, *Gonolobus barbatus* Kunth and *Lagenaria siceraria* (Molina) Standl. bear variations on the common name *tuch* (pp. 287–88). Also see p. 244, where *haz-ak* or *mamey* vine is used to treat gangrene and dysentery.

Metopium brownei (Jacq.) Urban   Anacardiaceae

Mayan name: *chechem*
Field Notes: Tree with yellow flowers in June and July. The fruit is reddish yellow. Grows to ten meters tall. **Uses:** To remove warts. Apply a drop of resin. All parts of the tree are a strong skin irritant, producing a reaction similar to that of poison ivy *(Rhus radicans).*

Roys (1931:234): The Spanish name is *grenadillo*. Although the plant is said to be a skin irritant, the wood is used in furniture construction.

Mimosa pudica L.   Leguminosae

Mayan name: *x mudz*
Field Notes: Shrub with fluffy white flowers and pink centers. **Uses:** To cure insomnia. Place three one-half-meter bunches below hammock under patient's head.

Roys (1931:267): A decoction of the leaves is employed in the treatment of lassitude, depression, and epilepsy. Juice is dripped into the eyes "to remove a film" (cataracts?). On p. 86, it is used to treat lassitude, "anyone who lacks heart."

Momordica charantia L.   Cucurbitaceae

Mayan Name: *chincha mora*   Spanish name: *cundeamor*
Field Notes: Vine with white flowers in January. Squash-like fruit has red pulp. **Uses:** 1) To fortify lungs. Boil two large handfuls of leaves and one liter of water with a little sugar. Drink one liter each day. 2) Seeds are edible.

Roys (1931:297): Called *yacunah-ak, cundeamor,* and love-vine. Edible, with yellow flowers.

Morinda yucatanensis Greenman   Rubiaceae

Spanish Name: *piña de culebra*
Field Notes: Vine, grows from runners. The fruit resembles a small pineapple, hence the name, "snake's pineapple." **Uses:** To get rid of warts. The plant is ground and applied to the wart.

Roys (1931:245) as *x-hoyen-cab, x-hoyoc:* The root supplied a scarlet dye. On p. 99 it is noted in the treatment of "twitching and convulsions or spasms in boys' eyes."

Nopalea sp.   Cactaceae

Mayan Name: *x pakam*   Spanish Name: *tunas*
Field Notes: Cactus with flat pads and red flowers. Grows to three meters tall. **Uses:** 1) To stop crying in children. Cut a pad into strips, then form strips into five crosses. Place one at each cardinal point around (or hanging from) hammock, with the fifth suspended above the child. 2) Edible.

Roys (1931:289): Several *Nopaleas* are mentioned under the name *tzacam.* *Tzacam-zotz* ("bat-cactus"?) is identified as *Nopalea inaperta.* The only use given is for *tzacam-kuch:* it is used to make a lotion to treat scabs.

Ocimum micranthum Willd.   Labiatae
Mayan Name: *x cacal tun*
Field Notes: Herb, grows to one-half meter tall. **Uses:** 1) To cure pimples. Boil a small bunch of leaves with an equal amount of *kanan* flowers and leaves in a cup of water until yellow, then wash affected area. 2) To remove small bits of matter that have blown into eyes. Placing a seed in the corner of the eye "attracts" the matter. 3) To cure dysentery. Soak five or six leaves in one liter of water, drink during the course of the day.

Roys (1931:221–22) as *x-cacal-tun, albahaca.* On pp. 46–48, it is noted as a treatment for dysentery and "blood in the feces." On p. 142, it is used to treat buboes.

Oxalis latifolia Kunth   Oxalidaceae
Mayan Name: *yala elel, yala eleh*
Field Notes: Herb, with blue flowers in April, May, and June, and deeply lobed leaves. Grows to one-half meter tall. **Uses:** 1) To cure external tumors, swellings, and sores. Pack leaves on affected area. Also applied to toothaches.

Roys (pp. 297–98): *yala-elel, acederilla* as *Oxalis yucatanensis* (Rose) Standl. or *O. latifolia* Kunth. States that Maya medical texts describe the former species as having yellow flowers. The root or the whole steamed plant is noted as a cure for various types of swellings and sores. Taken internally, the plant is a treatment for vomiting blood, "lassitude," and "rotten liver." Also, on p. 263, *matzab-kuch,* or "the *yala-elel* with a yellow flower" is identified as *O. yucatanensis.* This species is prescribed for "scab" and is an antidote for poison.

Parthenium hysterophorus L.   Compositae
Mayan Name: *pulmonia xiu*
Field Notes: Herb with small white flowers in January. Grows to one meter tall. **Uses:** To cure fever. Boil and drink a tea prepared with a large handful of leaves, a (liter) bottle of water, and some sugar.

Roys (1931:243) as *hauay, x-hauay, hauay-che:* Uses include remedies for headache, skin diseases, and falling hair. *Hauay-che* is also utilized in a decoction for treatment of swollen testicles, a stone in the bladder, blood in the urine, and sore eyes. On p. 21, the plant is noted as a component in postdelivery care.

Passiflora sp.   Passifloraceae
Mayan Name: *x po kinil*
Field Notes: Vine, with round purple flowers in the spring. **Uses:** To treat venereal sores. Apply the resin from the stem or the fruit to the affected area every day until healed.

Roys lists several *Passifloras,* with no use given for *P. ciliata* Ait. *(x-poch-kak)* on p. 277. *P. coriacea* Juss. *(xic-tzotz)* is used to treat some ailment of the eye (1931:295). Only *P. foetida* (1931:287) has a similar use. See next entry.

Passiflora foetida L. Passifloraceae

Mayan Name: *poch*

Field Notes: Vine, with white round flowers and round, red fruit. Fern-like leaflets around flower unite beneath the ovary. **Uses:** Edible fruit (?), applied to sores.

Roys (1931:287) as *tuu-boc, x-tu-can:* Applied to swellings, sores, and ringworm. *P. ciliata* Ait. as *x-poch-kak.*

Passiflora pulchella Kunth Passifloraceae

Mayan Name: *xic tzotz* Spanish Name: *alas del murciélago*

Field Notes: Vine. Said to have no flowers. The shape of the leaves resembles the wings of a bat, hence the name. There is "another type" with reddish leaves found in the highlands. **Uses:** To cure *xic,* or *golondrina* (pimples that appear in the armpit, which are "white when they appear." [Don Cósimo])

Roys (1931:295): *Passiflora coriacea* Juss. as *xik-tzotz.* Used for a type of eye ailment.

Pedilanthus itzaeus Millsp. Euphorbiaceae

Mayan Name: *yaax halal che*

Field Notes: Shrub, with a distinctive "zigzag" stem and red flowers in the rainy season. Grows to one meter tall. **Uses:** To protect against evil winds. Plant one plant in each corner of the yard and one in the center. Also, bury a cross made of cut pieces of the stem in the center.

Roys (1931:299) as *yax-halalche:* Multiple uses. An infusion of the gum is prescribed as a remedy for coughs and sores. The sap is applied to swellings. On p. 54, it is said to correct obstruction of "some organ, possibly the spleen."

Persea americana Miller Lauraceae

Mayan Name: *on* Spanish Name: *aguacate*

Field Notes: Tree, with shiny leaves, yellow flowers, and egg-shaped fruit with green-black peel and green flesh. **Uses:** 1) Edible fruit. 2) To cure rheumatism. Boil a one-meter section of bark in a bucket of water. Bathe in this once a day for three days. 3) To cure diarrhea. Boil six tender leaves in one liter of water. Prepare and drink tea four times a day. 4) To improve skin. Boil an onion with an avocado fruit in a liter of water. Wash face with mixture.

Roys (1931:271): Edible. A drink made from the seeds is used to treat diarrhea and bladder complaints. Leaves are used for skin eruptions. On p. 195, the seed of the avocado is a treatment for "sweet urine" (diabetes).

Petiveria alliacea L. Phytolaccaceae

Mayan Name: *pay che*

Field Notes: Tall herb, grows to one meter tall. **Uses:** Treatment for rheumatism. The leaves and root are soaked with the cooked fruit of *ch'it cuc* (*Catasetum maculatum* Kunth), and then the medicine is poulticed on to the affected area.

Roys (1931:274) as *pay-che, zorrillo:* Notes garlic-like or skunk-like smell. Root and leaves used for treating dysentery, head cold, and buboes.

Phaseolus atropurpureus DC.   Leguminosae

Mayan Name: *x punhut xiu*

Field Notes: Vine, with dark purple flowers in January. **Uses:** 1) To cure "green diarrhea" in children. Soak a bunch of leaves in one liter of water, then bathe child with solution. 2) Leaves are also used to make a purple dye for clothing. Not mentioned in Roys.

Phaseolus elegans Piper   Leguminosae

Mayan Name: *x cap xiu* See figure 27.

Field Notes: Vine, with green flowers in January. These turn purple at maturity. **Uses:** To cure external cancers. Chop equal parts of the plant and *hulcini* (an unidentified species). Pack on affected areas. The same mixture is used for all kinds of swellings.

Roys (1931:6): This species is noted in the treatment of phthisis.

Phyllanthus sp.   Euphorbiaceae

Mayan Name: *cancer kax*

Field Notes: Small herb, with white flowers. Said to be toxic when taken internally. Scarce. **Uses:** The leaves are ground, mixed with a little water, and applied to external cancers. The medicine should be prepared and used at night. Should not be used around children, as it is said to harm them.

Roys notes three *Phyllanthus* species, all with divergent names. *Phyllanthus conami* Swartz. and *Phyllanthus acuminatus* Vahl are used for buboes and skin eruptions (1931:274). *P. nobilis* (L.) Muell. is described as "ointment tree" (1931:268).

Piper sp.   Piperaceae

Mayan Name: *yax pelech che*

Field Notes: Shrub, with large white fruit (flowers) in July. Resembles *x makulan* (see next two *Piper* species). **Uses:** Cures headache. Soak equal parts of this plant and *roble (Ehretia tinifolia)* in a bucket of water from six in the evening to twelve at night. Then wash the patient's head with the medicine. One treatment should be sufficient to give relief.

Roys (1931:300): *yaax-ppehel-che* is identified as *Piper medium* Jacq. The crushed leaves of the plant are rubbed on the patient's head to cure headaches. The leaves are steeped and then used to treat a scalp complaint.

Piper amalago L.   Piperaceae

Mayan Name: *x makulan silvestre, x makulam silvestre*

Field Notes: Shrub, to five or six meters tall. **Uses:** To make a shampoo that prevents hair loss. Dry a kilo of leaves in the sun, then soak in a bucket of water for ten minutes.

Roys (1931:263): *Piper auritum* Kunth as *maculan, ix-maculan*. The leaves are toasted and then applied to sores.

Piper auritum Kunth   Piperaceae
Mayan Name: *makulan, makulam*   Spanish Name: *yerba santa*
See figure 28.
Field Notes: Tall tree with white flowers. **Uses:** 1) To smoke "like tobacco" (Don Tomás). Leaves are dried and smoked. 2) To wrap food to be cooked in a *pib*.

Roys (1931:263) as *x makulam*. Toasted leaves are applied to sores and used as a remedy for pleurisy. Compare previous two entries of other Piper species.

Piscidia piscipula (L.) Sargent   Leguminosae
Mayan Name: *habin, habim* See figure 29.
Field notes: Tree. **Uses:** 1) To cure a cough. Chew and swallow nine tender leaves with a bit of salt. 2) Wood used to build houses.

Roys (1931:242) *Piscidia piscipula* (L.) Sargent (*Piscidia erythrina* L.) (*Ichthyomethia communis* Blake) as *habin:* The wood is used in construction, the leaves are used in a bath for fever and asthma, and are taken internally for ringworm.

Plantago major L.   Plantaginaceae
Mayan Name: *llanten*
See figure 30.
Field Notes: Herb with very small flowers on erect spines. **Uses:** To cure headaches. Mash ten centimeters of seed-bearing flowering stalk. Apply to head.

Roys (1931:298) as *yanten, llanten:* Notes that the name seems to be a corruption of the Spanish name, and that the plant is considered to be a European importation, although a sixteenth-century account mentions the medicinal use of the plant. P. 20 notes the use of the plant in bringing on delayed menstruation. On p. 61, its seeds are noted as a treatment for dysentery, and on p. 68, it is mentioned as a treatment for burns.

Plumeria obtusa L.   Apocynaceae
Mayan Name: *nicte ch'om*   Spanish Name: *flor del zopilote*
Field Notes: Shrub, with sticky white sap. Grows to five meters tall. **Uses:** 1) To increase lactation and alleviate swellings of the breasts. Apply resin. 2) Resin is also used on blisters, calluses, and to relieve pain.

Roys (1931:270): The sap of *nicte-chom* is sedative and used on toothache and decayed teeth. Described as a large tree with white flowers, "resembling the *Flor de Mayo.*" It is not identified beyond the genus level. P. 68 notes the generic use of "any *Plumeria*" in the treatment of burns.

Porophyllum punctatum (Miller) Blake   Compositae
Mayan Name: *x pech' ukil*
Field Notes: Shrub with yellow flowers said to resemble *x tempula* (*Tagetes erecta*). **Uses:** The leaves are edible and are considered to be very healthful.

Roys (1931:275) as *x-pech-ukil, ek-puc-che, uk-che:* Leaves are used to kill lice and treat ulcers. On p. 159, the plant is poulticed onto "scab."

Portulaca oleracea L.   Portulacaceae
                                                  Spanish Name: *verdolaga*
Field Notes: Herb with yellow flowers. **Uses:** Edible leaves. Often boiled and served with eggs.

Roys (1931:220) as *cabal-chum, verdolaga.* On p. 296, *xucul, h-xucul, verdolaga,* is noted as a remedy for a variety of conditions, including convulsions, "pain in the heart," and spitting blood. P. 4 mentions its use in treating consumption.

Priva lappulacea (L.) Pers.   Verbenaceae
Mayan Name: *x opol*
Field Notes: Herb with tiny purple flowers and green fruit. **Uses:** To cure *xtusangas* (sores with white centers). Soak three cigarettes in a bucket of water with two handfuls of the leaves of the plant. Bathe sores with the medicine for two consecutive days.

Roys (1931:290) as *tzayuntzay:* No use is given. On p. 272, *oppol-che* (*Adenocalymna seleri* Loes.) is used to treat external infections.

Psidium guajava L.   Myrtaceae
Mayan Name: *pichi*   Spanish Name: *guayaba*
Field Notes: Tree has round green fruit with pink interior. Grows to four meters tall. **Uses:** 1) Edible fruit. 2) To cure diarrhea. Boil two branches of leaves in one liter of water, and drink once a day for two days. 3) The same decoction is used to wash and sooth skin irritations.

Roys (1931:276) as *guayaba:* The juice of fruit is noted as a cure for diarrhea, while a decoction of the leaves is a cure for asthma and coughs. P. 2 prescribes a decoction of the plant to induce perspiration.

Psittacanthus americanus (Jacq.) Mart.   Loranthaceae
Mayan Name: *kubem ba*
Field Notes: Shrub with flame-colored flowers in July and January. **Uses:** To heal swellings and inflammations. Mash leaves with a small amount of water and apply to affected areas.

Roys (1931:254) as *keb, x-keu:* Applied externally for buboes.

Rauwolfia heterophylla L.   Apocynaceae
Mayan Name: *cabal muc, caba muc*
Field Notes: Shrub, with white flowers and fruit that turns from red to black at maturity. Grows to one meter tall. **Uses:** To heal old sores in animals caused by worms. Apply a small amount of the freshly grated root with an equal amount of lime. The medicine is "more for animals than humans" (Don Tomás).

Roys (1931:220) as *cabal-muc:* Bark and sap are used for chronic sores, decayed teeth, and "sore eyes."

Rhoeo discolor (L'Her.) Hance   Commelinaceae
Mayan Name: *morado che, chac tzab*
Field Notes: Herb, with spiky leaves that are purple on one side, green on the other.

Yellow or white flowers in January. **Uses:** 1) To remove calluses. Apply resin each day until cured. 2) To remove "black" or "white" stains on face. Apply four or five times.

Roys (1931:233) as *chac-tsam:* It is taken internally for snakebite, poulticed on swellings, and boiled for "eruption of pustules." Flowers are said to be white. See also p. 27, where its use in treating snakebite is described, and p. 160, where it is noted in the treatment of "cimex-eruption" (smallpox).

Ricinus communis L.   Euphorbiaceae
Mayan Name: *sac koch, koch blanco*   Spanish Name: *guarumbo blanco*
See figure 31.
Field Notes: Tree, to two meters tall. **Uses:** 1) To cure fever. Apply leaves to upper body with a little coffee. Remove after one hour, "when the leaves are black and cooked [with the absorbed heat?]" (Don Tomás). Other versions—Apply leaves to upper body with VapoRub. To cure colds. Apply leaves to upper body with hearth ashes. 2) To cure worms. Grind seeds and drink five drops of oil three times a day. 3) Seeds are very oily and can be threaded on palm fibers and used as candles. The plant shares its common name with *Cecropia peltata.*

Roys (1931:255–56) as *x-koch, higuerilla:* Notes that more than one plant has this name. Leaves and beans are used on swellings and hemorrhoids, for pain in the bowels, and many other uses. The plant is noted as a remedy for constipation and anuria on p. 44.

Rivina humilis L.   Phytolaccaceae
Mayan Name: *sabac pox*
Field Notes: Herb with small white flowers in racemes and round, red fruit. **Uses:** 1) Skin irritations, including pimples, scrapes, and scratches. The leaves are ground and applied to the affected areas. 2) To cure *síis* (an aliment that results from sudden temperature changes). The leaves must be boiled in water, and then the patient bathes with the medicine when tepid.

Roys (1931:260) as *kuxub-can:* Used to treat snakebites, wounds, erysipelas, ringworm, fever, and epilepsy. See also p. 165. On p. 18, its berries are used in a remedy for delayed menstrual periods.

Ruellia nudiflora (Engelm. & Gray) Urban   Acanthaceae
Mayan Name: *x cabal yax nic, x camba yax nic*
Field Notes: Small herb with purple flowers in January. **Uses:** 1) To cure kidney pain caused by inflammation. Boil a small bunch of leaves with forty-five centimeters of the bark of *elemuyil (Malmea depressa)*. Drink one-third liter each day for three days. 2) Above decoction also used to treat backache.

Roys (1931:221): *Ruellia tuberosa* L. as *x-cabal-yaxnic.* Notes the multiplicity of names in the Maya medical texts. Plant is applied to swollen breasts and sore mouths. Other *Ruellia* species are mentioned on p. 313. The roots of these plants are remedies for broken or dislocated bones. The Maya name is dissimilar to the one I collected and is related to their use: *x-tzacal-bac.*

Salvia coccinea L.   Labiatae
Mayan Name: *chac lol, chac tzits*
Field Notes: Herb, with red flowers in January. Grows to one meter tall. **Uses:** 1)
Leaves are ground up and placed on sores to cure them. 2) To cure *ojo* in children:
Equal parts of this plant and *x cambal ikil che* (?) are boiled, cooled, and then
used to bathe child.
　　　Roys (1931:232) as *chac-tzitz:* Root, stalk, and leaves used for treating cavities
in teeth. See also p. 189.

Salvia micrantha Vahl   Labiatae
Mayan Name: *yerba buena xiu*
Field Notes: Small herb with purple flowers and green fruit. There are said to be
three "types" of the plant (species of *Salvia?*). **Uses:** To treat pimples. Boil about
four plants in a bucket of water and bathe in the medicine to cure. Not in Roys.
The only *Salvia* mentioned is *S. coccinea* (see previous entry). *Yerba buena* refers
to mint in other parts of Mexico.

Sapindus saponaria L.   Sapindaceae
                                                        Spanish Name: *jaboncillo*
Field Notes: Tree, with yellow flowers in February and small round fruit. Grows to
ten meters tall. **Uses:** 1) Sap is used to wash clothes. 2) To make a shampoo that
prevents hair loss. Soak one kilo of fruit in ten liters of water. Will foam up when
fruit is mashed.
　　　Roys (1931:309): *zihom, zihum* is "probably" *Sapindus saponaria* L. Used for
making soap. Seeds used for necklaces and rosaries.

Selenicereus donkelaarii (Salm.-Dyck)   Cactaceae
Mayan Name: *tzacam ak, kan choch*
Field Notes: Plant has white flowers in May and June. Said to grow up to twenty
meters tall. **Uses:** To cure rashes and eruptions in children's mouths. Boil fifteen
centimeters of plant with one liter of water. First wash child's mouth with two
leaves of *sac misib (Abutilon permolle),* then with cooled *tzacam ak* medicine.
Two treatments.
　　　Roys (1931:289) as *tzacam-ak:* No use is given. On p. 302, it appears as *zac-
bacel-can,* which is used for an assortment of skin ailments, as well as for headache,
convulsions, and snakebite. See also pp. 145–46 (treatment of tumors or ulcer),
and p. 165 (treatment for ringworm).

Sida acuta Burm.   Malvaceae
Mayan Name: *chichi be* See figure 32.
Field Notes: Small herb with yellow flowers in January. **Uses:** 1) To cure *garaspera*
(bad cough). Boil equal parts of *chichi be* and *x kuts cap* (?) with a little sugar in a
liter of water. Drink four teaspoons every four hours. 2) Leaves may be dried and
smoked "like marijuana" (Don Pedro). This practice is said to "dry out the brains"
and is considered unwise.

Roys (1931:236): Multiple uses for leaves including as a cure for asthma, fainting, headache, stomach complaints, and phthisis. On p. 179, it is noted as a remedy for ringworm.

Solanum americanum Miller   Solanaceae
Spanish Name: *yerba mora*

Field Notes: Herb, with white flowers with yellow centers. Grows to one meter tall. **Uses:** To cure burns. Chop leaves and apply juice to affected area. Not in Roys, but on p. 273 *S. nigrum* L. (as *yerba mora*) is applied to a variety of skin afflictions including buboes, abscesses, and swellings. On p. 28 it is prescribed for snakebite.

Solanum nudum Kunth   Solanaceae
Mayan Name: *sicli muc*   Spanish Name: *pepita de rana*

Field Notes: Shrub, with white flowers in January. Grows to one meter tall. **Uses:** To cure pimples that appear in clusters (shingles? ringworm?). Squeeze juice from fruit on affected area. Not in Roys, although an unidentified plant called *zicil-tab* (1931:309) is applied as a treatment for ringworm. Also see previous entry.

Solanum tequilense Gray   Solanaceae
Mayan Name: *parpera xiu*

Field Notes: Shrub, has white flowers with yellow centers in January. **Uses:** To cure *parpera* (swollen glands). Remove spines from fruit and cut in half. Soak in a glass of water for one hour, then gargle with medicine. Does not relieve fever, just the glands themselves. Not in Roys.

Spermacoce sp.   Rubiaceae
Mayan Name: *buy*

Field Notes: Herb with white flowers during the rainy season only. **Uses:** To cure fleshy growths in the eyes. One small plant is used to prepare each dose of medicine. The chopped fresh leaves are placed in a piece of material, then squeezed so that three or four drops fall into each eye. Should be done three or four times daily. When the medicine begins to burn your eye, you know that it is time to stop the treatment.

Roys lists two *Spermacoce* species, with very different names, and no given uses (1931:270, *S. verticillata* L.; p. 284, *S. tenuior*). On p. 219, *Serjania adiantoides* Radlk. as *buy, buy-ak;* a vine used to treat eye complaints.

Spermacoce tetraquetra A. Rich   Rubiaceae
Mayan Name: *buy*

Field Notes and Uses: as in previous number. Not in Roys.

Spilanthes filipes Greenman   Compositae
Mayan Name: *x koro xiu*

Field Notes: Herb with yellow flowers. **Uses:** Treatment for pimples (blackheads). The entire plant is boiled in three liters of water, and the affected area is bathed with the medicine. Not in Roys.

Stigmaphyllon ellipticum (Kunth) Juss.   Malpighiaceae
Mayan Name: *u xiu can, u lol can*   Spanish Name: *hierba de la culebra*
Field Notes: An herb; *u xiu can* means "snake's plant," and *u lol can* means "snake's flower." **Use:** The entire plant, including the roots, is ground up and applied to bites. Not in Roys, but on p. 222, an unidentified plant known as *x-can-ak* ("snake-vine") is mentioned as a treatment for "certain pustules" and sore eyes.

Tagetes erecta L.   Compositae
Mayan Name: *x tempula xiu, tempula*   Spanish Name: *flor de la muerte*
Field Notes: Herb with orange or yellow flowers. The familiar marigold. **Uses:** 1) To make a tonic for muscular cramps. Soak a thirty-centimeter clump in a bucket of water in the sun, leaving it there from 6:00 A.M. to 2:00 P.M., or until the liquid is "like tea" (Don Cósimo). Bathe each day with this medicine for three days. 2) Flowers are placed in cemeteries each year during the two Days of the Dead. The use of the plant for muscle aches is well known among Mexican-Americans (personal communications).
     Roys (1931:279–80): *T. erecta* L. (*T. patula* L.) as *x-puhuk, maceual-puhuk, pastora*. No use is given.

Talinum paniculatum (Jacq.) Gaertn.   Portulaceae
Mayan Name: *chupí* See figure 33.
Field Notes: Herb, with small red flowers and green fruit. Grows to one-half meter tall. **Uses:** To treat swellings and sores. Chop fresh leaves and plaster on with a little water. Apply three times a day. Not in Roys.

Talinum triangulare (Jacq.) Willd.   Portulaceae
Mayan Name: *dzum yahil, dzum yahih* See figure 34.
Field Notes: Herb, with pink flowers in January. Grows to one meter tall. **Uses:** To cure external tumors, swellings, and sores. Chop a handful each of *dzum yahil* and *yalah eleh* and plaster on affected area. Three days of treatments. Not in Roys, but on p. 315, *dzum-ya* or *dzum-yail* is tentatively identified as *Pereskia aculeata* Mill. The flowers are said to be white, yellow, or pinkish. The leaves are crushed and applied to swellings and tumefactions. Roys translates the name as literally meaning "that which reduces a swelling."

Tecoma stans (L.) Juss.   Bignoniaceae
Mayan Name: *x kan lol*
Field Notes: Shrub with yellow trumpet-shaped flowers and green fruit. The seeds are white. **Uses:** To treat diabetes. The leaves and flowers are boiled in a liter of water. The medicine is bitter, and a bit of sugar may be added for taste.
Roys (1931:251–52) as *x-kan-lol, tronadores:* The seeds are used for abdominal pains and "foul yellow stools." The latter is perhaps another example of the Doctrine of Signatures. The leaves are employed in the treatment of buboes and "other diseases."

Thevetia gaumeri Helmsl.   Apocynaceae
Mayan Name: *pisté*
Field Notes: Tree, with yellow-green flowers and ovoid fruit. Grows to five meters tall.
Uses: To deaden pain in cavities. Apply sap from fruit and leaves with a piece of cotton.

Roys (1931:214): *Thevetia peruviana* (Pers.) Standley as *acitz. Thevetia gaumeri* is called *campanilla, cabalonga* and is said to have poisonous seeds. On p. 79, *T. nereifolia* Juss. is mentioned in the treatment of chills.

Thouinia paucidentata Radlk.   Sapindaceae
Mayan Name: *x kan chunup* See figure 35.
Field Notes: Shrub, with yellow flowers in May. Grows to five meters tall. **Uses:** To cure diarrhea. Boil two or three small pieces of bark with one liter of water. Drink a small amount. Repeat if necessary.

Roys (1931:251): The root cures snakebite (see also p. 23), headache (see also p. 109), and fainting spells.

Tridax procumbens L.   Compositae
Mayan Name: *sac sahun, x akab xiu*
Field Notes: Herb with opposite leaves and yellow flowers. **Uses:** To frighten away night birds (owls). The birds fly over the roofs of houses and make children cry. You must bathe the children to make them stop. The plant is boiled in water, and then used to bathe the children. See also *Blechum pyramidatum.* A second voucher of the same plant is called *sac sahun* and is used the same way, except that the offending bird is described as a large and gray bird with yellow eyes, feet like hooves (?), and a red mouth.

Roys (1931:214): *akab-xiu* as *Blechum pyramidatum* (Lam.) Urban. Used for coughs, bleeding, chills and fever.

Urechites andriuexii Muell. Arg.   Apocynaceae
Mayan Name: *ixim che*
Field Notes: Shrub, grows to three or four meters tall. The fruit is white and appears in August. **Uses:** For women's cramps and hemorrhages "when her period goes on too long" (Don Tomás). Two handfuls of leaves are boiled in a half-bucket of water. The patient is bathed with the medicine.

Roys (1931:249): Notes that two plants in what is now the Belizean National Herbarium were given the name *ixim-che: Casearia nitida* L. and *Citharexylum schottii* Greenm. The Maya texts give *ic-che* as a synonym, which is taken for cramps.

Urera caracasana (Jacq.) Griseb.   Urticaceae
Mayan Name: *lal*   Spanish Name: *ortiga*
See figure 36.
Field Notes: Tree, to ten meters tall. **Uses:** 1) To cure body aches. Warm two leaves, then apply to painful area. Two treatments. 2) To cure stomach/bladder pains. Grind four to five large leaves and drink with a small glass of water.

Roys (1931:261): *Urera caracasana* (Jacq.) Griseb. (*Urera microcarpa* Wedd.) as *laal, la, ortiga*. Leaves are used for aching bones, loss of strength, chills, fever, and dysentery. The sap is applied to the forehead and soles of the feet to stop nosebleeds.

Zanthoxylum sp.   Rutaceae
Mayan Name: *tamcaz che, x tancaz che*
Field Notes: Tree, with small purple flowers. Fruit in pods "like beans" (Don Pedro).
Uses: 1) For headache and other body aches, including rheumatism. The root is scraped, and the peelings are soaked in alcohol. Then, the medicine is rubbed on the patient's head. 2) To keep evil winds away. A small piece of a branch is placed beneath the person's hammock or carried in their bag as an amulet.

Roys (1931:283): *Zanthoxylum fagara* as *tamcaz-ché, tancaz-ché, uole*. It is used to treat flatulence, convulsions, and erysipelas. *Z. caribaeum* Lam. (1931:309) is used for headaches, as well as dysentery and diarrhea.

Unidentified Species
　contrahierba
　cocuite, sac yap = Gliricidia sepium ? (Kaua ms.)
　belladonna
　x pop che
　necina
　x chum ak
　contrahierba
　hulcini
　yax uxh
　kah yuk = Astrocasia phyllanthoides ?
　x kul kinil = Porophyllum ?
　yax uxh
　poch—not the *Passiflora* with same common name
　x pulmonayaxiu

Plants with Uses Similar to Roys (1931)

The scientific binomial appears in the first column.

The second column contains the use(s) I collected that also appear in Roys' (1931) *The Ethno-Botany of the Maya.*

Scientific Binomial	Use
Annona glabra L.	Edible fruit
Annona squamosa L.	Edible fruit, fever
Asclepias curassavica L. (figure 4)	R. Abscesses K. Toothache (painkiller)
Bauhinia divaricata L. (figure 5)	R. Pleurisy K. Sore throat
Bixa orellana L.	Condiment, coloring agent, treatment for red eruptions (measles, smallpox)
Blechum pyramidatum (Juss.) Urban (figure 6)	Fever
Brosimum alicastrum Swartz	Edible fruit, coughs
Bunchosia swartziana Griseb. (*Bunchosia glandulosa* (Cav. DC.)	Convulsions brought on by evil winds (epilepsy?)
Bursera simaruba (L.) Sarg. (figure 8)	Skin ailments, snakebite, fever
Byrsonima crassifolia (L.) Kunth (figure 9)	Edible fruit
Calea urticifolia (Mill.) DC.	Skin ailments
Capsicum annuum L.	Edible fruit
Carica papaya L.	Swellings, snakebite
Casimiroa tetrameria Millsp.	Fever
Cassia villosa Miller (figure 12)	Skin ailments
Catasetum maculatum Kunth (figure 13)	Swellings, sores
Cecropia peltata L. (*Cecropia obtusa* Trecul)	Diuretic
Cedrela mexicana M. Roem	Earache, house construction
Citrus aurantium (Christm.) Swingle (*Citrus amara* Link)	R. Buboes K. Bruises
Cnidoscolus chayamansa Mc Vaugh (figure 16) (*Jatropha aconitifolia* Mill.) (*Jatropha urens* L.)	Edible leaves, purgative qualities
Coccoloba uvifera L.	Edible fruit
Colubrina greggii S. Watson (figure 17)	Painkiller
Cordia dodecandra Kunth	Edible fruit
Croton flavens L.	R. Snakebite K. Bucal sores
Croton humilis L.	R. Sores, buboes K. Warts
Diphysa carthagenensis Jacq. (figure 21)	Dysentery R. Inflamed eye K. Evil eye

Scientific Binomial	Use
Dorstenia contrajerva L.	Stomach problems

Erythrina standleyana Krukoff
   (*Erythrina americana* Mill.)
   (*Erythrina coralloides* Mocq. & Sesse)
	Eye complaints

Eupatorium odoratum L. (figure 23)
   (*Eupatorium conyzoides* Mill.)
   (*Trixis radialis* [L.] Kuntze.)
	R. Blood in the urine, malaria, gonorrhea
	K. Retention of urine

Euphorbia schlectendalii Boiss.	Skin complaints
Gossypium hirsutum L.	R. Asthma K. Coughs
Guazuma ulmifolia Lam.	R. Abdominal pains, cramps K. Delivery pains, hastens birth, painkiller
Hamelia patens (Jacq.)	Skin ailments
Hibiscus poeppigii (Sprengel) Garcke (*Hibiscus tubiflorus* DC.)	Swellings, inflammations
Jatropha gaumeri Greenman (figure 25)	Dysentery, purgative
Leucaena leucocephala (Lam.) de Witt	Ingesting plant causes animals' tails to fall out
(*Leucocephala glauca* (L.) Benth.	R. Does not note that seeds are edible
Lonchocarpus longistylus Pittier (figure 26)	Ceremonial wine
Metopium brownei (Jacq.) Urban	Skin irritant
Momordica charantia L.	Edible
Ocimum micranthum Willd.	Dysentery R. Buboes K.Pimples
Oxalis latifolia Kunth	Skin ailments
Passiflora foetida L.	Sores
Persea americana Miller	Edible fruit, diarrhea, skin treatment

Piscidia piscipula (L.) Sargent (figure 29)
   (*Piscidia erythrina* L.)
   (*Ichthyomethia communis* Blake)
	House construction
	R. Asthma
	K. Coughs

Psidium guajava L.	Edible fruit, diarrhea
Psittacanthus americanus (Jacq.) Mart.	R. Buboes, sores K. Swellings, inflammations
Rauwolfia heterophylla L.	Sores
Rhoeo discolor (L'Her) Hance	Skin ailments
Ricinus communis L. (figure 31)	R. Pain in the bowels K. Worms
Rivina humilis L.	Skin ailments
Salvia coccinea L.	R. Cavities K. Sores, painkiller
Sapindus saponaria L.	Soap
Selenicereus donkelaarii (Salm.-Dyck)	Skin ailments
Sida acuta Burm. (figure 32)	Coughs
Urera caracasana (Jacq.) Griseb. (figure 36.) (*Urera microcarpa* Wedd.)	Stomach complaints R. Aching bones K. Body aches

Glossary

The Mayan and Spanish terms that appear in this book, apart from plant names, are listed alphabetically. Definitions are drawn from dictionaries, the references cited, and personal experience. Since this glossary is designed for English speakers, *Ch* is not treated as a separate letter, as in Spanish. The *(x-)* prefix indicates the feminine form in Yucatec Mayan words. The Spanish words suffixed by *(-a)* indicate the feminine form and those suffixed by *(-o)* indicate the masculine form.

aire	air or cold that enters the body and causes illness.
almud	measurement equal to four kilos.
alux	small beings who have human forms and can be mischievous if not propitiated with food. Some curers consider them to be the helpers of the *balams*.
balam	literally, "jaguar"; class of supernaturals who appear to curers in dreams and teach practitioners their skills. They are also, more generally, considered to be the guardians of Mayan villages, but their behavior toward humans may be capricious or punishing.
balche	ceremonial wine made from *Lonchocarpus longistylus* Pittier. Also, the tree itself.
bilis	literally bile or biliousness. A "hot" disease brought on by excessive emotion, especially anger.
calentura	fever.
ch'a chaac	rainmaking ceremony.
chaparrito(-a)	a person short in stature, "runt."
ch'en zahi	practitioner who treats sprains and dislocations.
chubasco	tropical rainstorm.
comadre	mother or godmother (with respect to each other); close friend; neighbor (female).
comadrona	midwife.
consultorio	dispensary.
curandero(-a)	curing practitioner.
defensa	magical defense; guard.
delantal	apron; a part of traditional male dress (obsolete?).
(x) dzadzac	herbalist.
ejido	public land; community property; commons
frío	cold; weak; sterile (a woman); any of a complex of debilitating diseases (usually in women).
guardian	custodian of an archaeological or historical site.
(x) h-men	Maya curers who utilize *sastuns* in their practices.
INAH	Instituto Nacional de Antropología e Historia.
INI	Instituto Nacional Indigenista.
kaxbaac	bonesetters. See p. 158
kex	ceremony performed to change bad luck.

kuilob kaaxob	guardians of the uncultivated forest.
limpio	cleansing ritual, in which the patient is "swept" of evil, usually with leaves and branches of *Bunchosia* species.
loh	lustrative ceremony that protects a village.
maldad	evil; wickedness.
maleficio	curse; spell; witchcraft. Evil done to someone.
masa	dough made from ground corn, lime, and water.
mesas	altars prepared for Maya ceremonies.
milpa	slash-and-burn agricultural field where corn, beans, and other crops are grown. These may be located at some distance from villages.
monte	uncultivated land; forest.
ojo	evil eye.
ojo de agua	spring.
partera(-o)	midwife.
pasmo	literally a chill, but used to refer to a "cold" sickness or complex of ailments.
pepitas	squash seeds.
pib	underground oven used in preparing ritual foodstuff.
pibiwah	special tortillas prepared in an underground oven.
posada	inn.
primicia	"first fruit" ceremony.
pulyah	male sorcerer.
rancho	isolated homestead.
remojar	to soak; to steep. Plant medicines are often prepared this way.
sabucam	carrying bag, traditionally made from plant fibers, but also made of plastic.
sancochar	to boil. Plant medicines are often prepared this way.
santiaguar	blessing; sanctifying ceremony.
sastun	divining crystal.
semejante	fellow man.
sobador(-a)	one who practices massage. Sobadora is a synonym (euphemism?) for a (female) midwife.
solar	houseyard; house plot.
sortilegio	witchery; sorcery.
tigrillo	small cat; ocelot.
tok	flint; arrows of the *Balams*.
uayoob	transforming witches.
utzkil a bac	bone-fixer.
vientos	evil winds, often personified, that bring sickness.
vientos malos	evil winds.
x-hiikab	female massage practitioner.
x-ilah-kohan	midwife; female curer.
xiu	herb; plant.
yerba	herb; plant.
yerbatero(-a)	herbalist.
yuntziloob	agricultural deities.
zip	class of supernaturals who are masters of the deer.

References Cited

Arvigo, Rosita. 1994. *Sastun*. New York: Harper Collins Publications.

Barrera Vásquez, Alfredo, and Silvia Rendón. 1948. *El libro de los libros de Chilam Balam*. México, D.F.: Fondo de Cultura Económica.

Behar, Ruth. 1993. *Translated Woman*. Boston: Beacon Press.

Berlin, Brent, Dennis Breedlove, and P. H. Raven. 1973. "General Principals of Classification and Nomenclature in Folk Biology." *American Anthropologist* 75:214–42.

Breedlove, Dennis E., and Robert Laughlin. 1993. *The Flowering of Man: A Tzotzil Botany of Zinacantán*. Washington, D.C.: Smithsonian Institution Press.

Bricker, Victoria R., and Helga-Maria Miram, trans. and eds. 2002. *An Encounter of Two Worlds: The Book of Chilam Balam of Kaua*. Tulane University, Middle American Research Institute, Publication 68. New Orleans: Tulane University.

Burns, Allan F. 1983. *An Epoch of Miracles: Oral Literature of the Yucatec Maya*. Austin: University of Texas Press.

Covarrubias, Miguel. 1957. *Indian Art of México and Central America*. New York: Alfred A. Knopf.

Cuevas, Benjamin. 1913. *Plantas medicinales de Yucatán y guía médica práctica doméstica*. Mérida: Imprenta de la lotería del estado de Yucatán.

Dondé, Joaquín, and Juan Dondé. 1907. *Apuntes sobre las plantas de Yucatán*. Mérida: Imprenta de la lotería del estado de Yucatán.

Edmonson, Munro S., and Victoria R. Bricker. 1985. "Yucatecan Maya Literature," pp. 44–63. In *Supplement to the Handbook of Middle American Indians*, vol. 3, edited by Victoria R. Bricker. Austin: University of Texas Press.

Elmendorf, Mary. 1976. *Nine Mayan Women*. Cambridge, Mass.: Schenkman Publishing Company.

Emmart, Emily, ed. 1940. *The Badianus Manuscript*. Baltimore: Johns Hopkins Press.

Foster, George. 1994. *Hippocrates' Latin American Legacy: Humoral Medicine in the New World*. Langhorne, Pa.: Gordon & Breach.

Guerra, Francisco. 1952. *Libellus de Medicinalibus Indorum Herbis*. México, D.F.: Editorial Vargas Rea y El Diario Español.

Hanks, William F. 1996. "Exorcism and the Description of Participant Roles." In *Natural Histories of Discourse*, edited by Michael Silverstein and Greg Urban, pp. 160–200. Chicago: University of Chicago Press.

Hernández, Francisco. 1959. Trans. José Rojo Navarro. *Historia Natural de Nueva España*. México, D.F.: Universidad Nacional Autónoma de México.

Ixil, Chilam Balam de. Ms. Copy with additions and annotations by Frans Blom and Ralph Roys. Latin American Library at Tulane University.

Kaua, Chilam Balam de. Ms. Copy with annotations by Ralph Roys. Latin American Library at Tulane University.

Landa, Diego de. 1938. *Relacíon de las cosas de Yucatán.* Introduction by Alfredo Barrera Vásquez. Mérida, Yucatán: E. G. Triay e hijos, imps.

———. 1941. *Landa's Relación de las Cosas de Yucatán: A Translation.* Translated and edited by Alfred M. Tozzer. Papers of the Peabody Museum of American Archaeology and Ethnology, vol. 18. Cambridge, Mass.: Harvard University.

Laughlin, Robert. 1976. *Of Wonders Wild and New: Dreams from Zinacantán.* Smithsonian Contributions to Anthropology, 22. Washington, D.C.: Smithsonian Institution Press.

———. 1977. *Of Cabbages and Kings: Tales from Zinacantán.* Smithsonian Contributions to Anthropology, 23. Washington, D.C.: Smithsonian Institution Press.

Manuscritos de Tekax y Nah. 1981. México, D.F.: Grupo Dzibil.

Martínez, Maximino. 1933. *Las plantas medicinales de México.* México, D.F.: Ediciones Botas.

McGee, Jon R. 1990. *Life, Ritual, and Religion among the Lacandon Maya.* Belmont, Calif.: Wadsworth Publishing Company.

Mena Ms. Maya Ms. of medical texts, "probably eighteenth century," according to Ralph Roys. Transcribed by a Sr. Mena for William E. Gates. Latin American Library at Tulane University.

Mendieta, Rosa, and Silvia del Amo. 1981. *Plantas medicinales del estado de Yucatán.* Jalapa: Instituto Nacional de Investigaciones Sobre Recursos Bíoticos.

Press, Irwin. 1975. *Tradition and Adaptation: Life in a Modern Yucatan Maya Village.* Westport, Conn.: Greenwood Press.

———. 1977. "The Urban Curandero." In *Culture, Disease, and Healing,* edited by David Landy, pp. 454–64. New York: Macmillan.

Redfield, Robert. 1941. *The Folk Culture of Yucatan.* Chicago: University of Chicago Press.

———. 1950. *A Village That Chose Progress: Chan Kom Revisited.* Chicago: University of Chicago Press.

Redfield, Robert, and Margaret Park Redfield. 1940. "Disease and Its Treatment in Dzitas, Yucatan," pp. 49–82. In *Contributions to American Anthropology and History,* vol. 6. Washington, D.C.: Carnegie Institution of Washington.

Redfield, Robert, and Alfonso Villa Rojas. 1934. *Chan Kom: A Maya Village.* Publication 448. Washington, D.C.: Carnegie Institution of Washington.

———. 1962. *Chan Kom: A Maya Village.* Chicago: University of Chicago Press. An abridged edition.

Reed, Nelson. 1964. *The Caste War in Yucatán.* Stanford, Calif.: Stanford University Press.

Roeder, Beatrice. 1988. *Chicano Folk Medicine from Los Angeles, California.*

Berkeley: University of California Press.

Romano, Octavio. 1965. "Charismatic Medicine, Folk Healing, and Folk Saint-hood." *American Anthropology* 67:1151–73.

Roys, Ralph. 1931. *The Ethno-Botany of the Maya.* Middle American Research Institute, Publication 2. New Orleans: Tulane University.

———. 1965. *Ritual of the Bacabs.* Norman, Okla.: University of Oklahoma Press.

———. 1976. *The Ethno-Botany of the Maya,* edited by Sheila Cosminsky. Philadelphia: Institute for the Study of Human Issues.

Sahagún, Fr. Bernardino de. 1975. *General History of the Things of New Spain.* Translated and edited by Arthur Anderson and Charles Dibble. Book 11. Santa Fe: School of American Research.

Schele, Linda, and Mary Ellen Miller. 1986. *The Blood of Kings: Dynasty and Ritual in Maya Art.* Fort Worth: Kimball Art Museum.

Sotuta Ms. 1928. Maya medical text. Copy with transcription, translation, and notes by Ralph Roys. Latin American Library at Tulane University.

Standley, Paul C. 1920–26. *Trees and Shrubs of Mexico.* Contributions from the United States National Herbarium. Vol. 23. Parts 1–5. Washington, D.C.: Smithsonian Institution.

———. 1930. *Flora of Yucatan.* Chicago: Field Museum of Natural History.

Steggerda, Morris. 1941. *Maya Indians of Yucatan.* Publication 531. Washington, D.C.: Carnegie Institute of Washington.

———. 1943. "Some Ethnological Data Concerning One Hundred Yucatecan Plants." Washington, D.C.: Government Printing Office.

Tedlock, Barbara. 1982. *Time and the Highland Maya.* Albuquerque: University of New Mexico Press.

Villa Rojas, Alfonso R. 1945. *The Maya of East Central Quintana Roo.* Publication 559. Washington, D.C.: Carnegie Institution of Washington.

Vogt, Evon Zartman. 1976. *Tortillas for the Gods: A Symbolic Analysis of Zinacanteco Rituals.* Cambridge: Harvard University Press.

Yerbas y hechicerías del Yucatán. Spanish Ms. Possibly the original *Libro del Judio.* Latin American Library at Tulane University.

Index of Plants by Families

Index